Kindle Me

The Ultimate Book about how to use ' Amazon's Kindle '*

By

Michael Haridy

Copyright

ME Text Publishing
ebooks@metextpublishing.com

ISBN 13: 978-1469900629
ISBN 10: 1469900629

First eBook Edition: December 2011

Contents

Prologue

In the beginning ...

I had no intention to write a book about an ebook reader . I hated ebooks, or let me say.. I did not appreciate the concept of ebooks . I loved, and still love in a way, the feel of real paper books; touching the pages , smelling the ink of the printed pages , flicking through a book in your hands is a pleasure in itself .

To travel or go on holidays carrying books, and I love to have more than one book with me most of the time, is a heavy load to carry. At the same time, my children and friends had with them more books than me and carried no weight at all.

I was surrounded and attacked visually and verbally by them. We argued about whether I should have an eReader . They repeated the same points; The eReader is light to carry, easy to handle, and easy to read from. They just repeated the same argument many many times . Within their Kindle which they carry , sometimes even in their pocket , they can have thousands of books or more ... and yes, they have it with them all the time!

One friend of mine who I promised not to name, loves to go to the toilet with a book! . He can't do 'you know what' without reading a book at the same time. Now, he tells me , he goes in there with his Kindle in his hand . He selects a suitable book to match his mood from the many books he has in his Kindle, and enjoys his reading whilst doing his deed!

* * *

In the end I surrendered…

It happened while I was on holiday, and had run out of books to read. I was edgy. In fact , everyone was trying to avoid me because of my attitude. So, my son came to me with his Kindle in his hand and said ..

' Here it is .. Just try it !'

He showed me how to use it to read . I looked at his collection of books and said ..

' No thanks , there is nothing for me to read there! I don't like what you read!'

He smiled and said

' What you want to read?'

' You don't have it there' I replied.

He smiled again and said

' Just tell me what you fancy reading now '

' Why?!'

' Just tell me ? '

So I mentioned a couple of books I knew were recently released and are not available yet in my local bookshop , just to tease him and make him leave me in peace . He started typing on his kindle and in few minutes gave me back the kindle and said:

' Here is one of the books you want . I got it for you . It is my gift . Calm down now and enjoy reading it '

In those few minutes he had downloaded from Amazon the book I was waiting for and had it on his kindle .

That was the start of my journey with the eReader Amazon's Kindle . From that day I was wired . I had my own kindle and it is with me most of the time now.

In fact I was was so hooked on my kindle that, as I usually do, I

talked about it to everyone, even in my emails to my friends and coworkers in the writing field. I think somehow I overdid it .
One day, a dear friend of mine said:
  ' Why don't you write a book about it instead of talking about it!
'

So I did....

How to read this book ?!

When I was asked to do this book about the ' Kindle ' I accepted on one condition: That the book will be a collection of the most useful information for someone who already has or is planning to purchase a Kindle.

So 'Kindle ME !' came to be ' the collection of the information I always wanted to have with me on my Kindle '.

It is a collection of information to enrich your usage of your Kindle .Not every piece of information may be what you are after now. But believe me, you may need it sometime in the future.

So, I decided to write FOUR BOOKS under one cover .

You go to the book you need, when you need it. But , if you are a fanatic and you want to know everything under the sun about your Kindle , you are welcome to read it all!

Book ONE : is about the history of ebooks and ereaders . It is a journey into the past in which the vision of few individuals changed the way we impart and receive knowledge . It is a journey through the history of the ereader.

Book TWO : is all about the basics . You have a Kindle and want to use it now. If you are an impatient individual and you want to start reading your first ebooks in a few minutes , this will show you how!

But if you want to grasp all the basics of how to use every aspect of your Kindle , you will find the answers there too .

Book THREE : it is free for all! Millions of free ebooks out there for you to read with your Kindle , and in this book , you will learn how to get them easily . Many ebooks on the market today have nothing else in them but the information you get from this book . This book is your complete guide on how to get to all the free ebooks available in the market today .Enjoy !

Book FOUR : This is a real gem! The information in this book took a lot of research to find and collect from the ever expanding world wide web.

This book contains some of the information no one has told you about; Like the hidden features of Kindle, it will enrich your usage of your Kindle . It will make the Kindle more than a Kindle!

It includes '10 things you need to know' , '10 features you don't know about' , '10 more ways to use your Kindle that no one told you about ' , 'how to do many things with your Kindle the easy way ' , and finally an important section about how to keep up to date with the latest information about Kindle - ' The best Kindle websites and blogs ' .

' Kindle ME ! ' is four books in one book . It takes your hand and slowly introduces you to the unbelievable world of Kindle . It is a magical world because Kindle is a superb eReader - one of the best , if not the best eReader on the market today. You can use your Kindle in more ways than just an eReader. It has many hidden features and ' Kindle ME !' will guide you through it.

So I hope you enjoy your journey with your Kindle as much as I enjoyed writing it !!

" If what you did yesterday
Still seems great today,
Then your goals for tomorrow
Are not big enough. "

Michael Hart

Book ONE

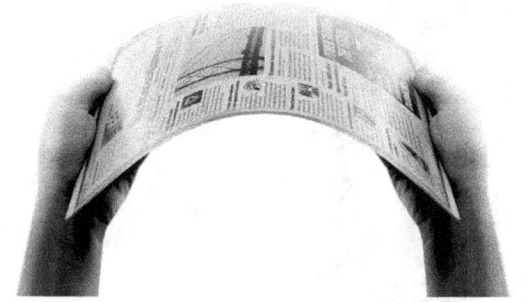

In The Beginning !

The History

ALL Started here !

The FIRST eBook !

His mother was Cryptanalyst during World War II , his father was an accountant , both with high IQ . In 1958 his family relocated to Urbana , Illinois , and his father and mother become college professors . His mother in Shakespearean studies and his father in mathematics education .

He attended the University of Illinois and graduated in just two years ! . He was also , briefly , a street musician !

He name is MICHAEL HART .

During Hart's time at the University of Illinois , the university computer center gave him a user's account on its computer system . Although the focus of computer use , in those days , tended to be data processing . Hart was aware that the mainframe computer was connected to a network with other universities in USA , which was the staring point of what become today INTERNET . Hart thought of the network as a machine for information distribution .

So, the story of the first ever EBOOK started .

It was the 4 of July , 1971 , when his account was created , in his way home after watching fireworks that evening he stopped at a grocery store to pickup some packaged food to munch on while using for the computer . The grocery shop owner was giving free , a copy of United States Declaration of Independence to its customers .

In that evening he typed the text into the computer . He was going to transmit it to his friends through the new , just added to the network , the E-MAIL system . But , he remembered the warning he received when he was given the access to the computer network that it was unacceptable to transmit an email , in those days ! , To numerous people at once via email because it may crash the whole system . So , he made the text available though the download function in the system instead .
That was the FIRST EBOOK ever to be put on the network system !

… And that was the beginning of Project GUTENBERG ! .

Hart began uploading text copies of classics books ; The Bible , Shakespeare ,Homer , Mark Twain ; on the network system for everyone to download for free from his Project Gutenberg site !

By 1987 , he had typed in total 313 books , and through the university of Illinois PC User Group , he was able to recruit volunteers and set up an infrastructure of mirror sites and mailing lists . The project was able to grow much more rapidly .

And as he wrote : the mission for the project were … .
" Encourage the creation and distribution of ebooks "
" Give as many ebooks to as many people as possible "

He supported himself by doing odd jobs and solicit donations for the project . He used to say to his friends .. " I know that sounds odd to most people , but I just never bought into the money system all that much . I never spent it when I got it . It's all a matter of perspective ".

He was a unique man . He had few possessions . He used home remedies rather than seeing doctors . He fixed his home and kept his old car going by repairing it himself . He build his own computers , stereos , and other gear from discarded components .

Michael Hart spent his all lifetime digitising literature from the pillars of books he staked in his house in Urbana , led a life of near poverty , basically lived off cans of beans . All the money he earned as adjunct professor at University of Illinois gave to Project Gutenberg .

Michael Hart died on September 6 , 2011 of heart attack at his home while working on his computer .

He could have been a billionaire by now if he patented and trademarked the concept of " ebooks " . He is been asked that question " Why didn't he do that ? ".

He answer was simple …

* * *

" In fact , I did think of patenting and trademarking ebooks , but I will have to honestly say that I wanted to change the world more than I am interested in profiting from such change "

....

We dedicate this book to him . Michael Hart changed our world and consciously decided not to profit from it . He gave us the eBook and Gutenberg Project . What a great human being he was !.

Now , HOW to read it !

The FIRST eReader !

E-books appeared on the web, easily shared and stored on a hard drive or storage disk, and quickly began to proliferate.

Early e-books were generally written in specialty areas, intended to be documents that only small groups might share, and therefore were few and far between. Their subject matter ranged from technical manuals for cutting-edge hardware and manufacturing techniques... to material "not suited for minors"... and everywhere in-between.

This fractured market of independents and specialty authors created a lack of consensus on the best way to package, sell, or read e-books.

Numerous e-book formats emerged and proliferated, some

supported by major software companies (like Adobe's PDF format), and others supported by independent and open-source programmers. Multiple readers naturally followed multiple formats, most of them in only one format, and thereby fragmenting the e-book market even more. The result was a lack of an overriding voice with the public regarding e-books, which kept e-books from becoming a mainstream product.

E-books continued to gain in their own underground markets. Many e-book publishers began distributing books that were in the public domain, or that were simply old and hard-to-find. At the same time, authors with books that were not accepted by their publisher began to strike out on their own, offering the books online so they could be seen by others. Unofficial (and occasionally unauthorised) catalogs of books became available over the web, and sites devoted to e-books began spreading the word to the public.

One of the first genres to become successful in the e-book field was that of the romance story. Romance novels were perfect for e-books, the genre already considered a "guilty pleasure" by most of the public, due to its oft-ridiculed and notoriously salacious content. E-book romances were easy to shop for and buy from the privacy of your home, and just as easy to read without revealing your guilty pleasure to others. Unbeknownst to the rest of the world, romance e-books had become a quiet success.
Libraries began to pay attention to e-books in 1998 when NetLibrary, a Colorado-based firm began to provide content. In 2002, they were purchased by OCLC (Online Computer Library Center, Inc.) who continues to provide content to libraries today.

The major publishing companies finally took notice of the e-book movement around 2001. The publishers, at first frightened of the capabilities of the new medium in much the same way as the music industry was against the MP3, are now following the music industry's example in trying to better understand, and ultimately take advantage of, the new e-book formats. They have established online stores and partnered with e-reader manufacturers to establish themselves in the e-book market. Concurrently, electronics hardware manufacturers are working on dedicated e-book readers, also hoping to capitalise on the e-book movement.

With all of this activity by major publishers and electronics companies alongside independents, new selling models are being developed, formats are beginning to homogenise, dedicated reading hardware is now available, and thanks to the Internet, e-books are achieving global distribution. Today, e-books are spawning new e-publishing houses, electronics manufacturers are releasing more e-book readers designed for the masses, and software designers are creating new reader applications for portable electronics gear like handheld computers, smartphones and game consoles. Let's not forget audio books as a form of electronic book. Busy, on-the-move readers can load a book in audio format onto their portable equipment and enjoy someone reading their favourite book them.

A company called E Ink recently introduced a new display technology, e-ink, which mimics the look of paper better than any other display technology. Its introduction into the latest reading devices has been hailed by many consumers as being far superior to LCD displays.

Then Oprah got involved - announcing that Amazon's Kindle e-book reader was her favorite gadget - and e-books met popular culture. Amazon couldn't keep enough Kindle's in stock to meet the demand. Sony also introduced a portable reader using the same e-ink display. The Sony PRS505 with it's amazing 6 inch screen was soon a crowd pleaser.

When you used to think of an ebook, you envisioned an eBook as an electronic version of a printed book available to view on a PC, Smart-Phone, E-Reader and other platforms. While that still remains true, you have a new breed of writers that are exclusively writing ebooks instead of tradition print media. For one big reason they do this, is writing an ebook costs nothing but time, and any copy of the book you sell you get a small profit, others choose to give the books away for free for promotion of a business or service.

Other Ebook authors such as Rhiannon Frater develop online blogs that compile books from entries and then form ebooks from them building a community of steady readers coming to the site every day to read.

The Resurgence of Ebooks has only been very prevalent for the last five years, due to the success of E-Readers from being a fringe gadget, to a main stream success. Also, do not discount the rise of mobile computing, such as Netbooks and Slate/Tablet PCS such as the iPad, Google Slate, HP Hurricane and others draw in more attention to portable media and ebooks.

Here a Brief History of eBooks

1998: The first eBook readers appear in the market: The Softbook and Gemstar's Rocket eBook Reader (pic).

2000: Stephen King's horror novel, Ride the Bullet, is released only as an eBook (at first).

* * *

2003: EBooks stumble as demand remains poor and paper books remain a steadfast favourite; Gemstar closes its doors in July, Barnes & Noble stops selling eBooks at its online store. Critics say the eBooks trend will not last.

2004: Sony releases the Librié, the first eBook reader to utilise eInk (electronic ink) technology. Gone is the annoying glare from backlit screens in earlier eBook readers or on PDAs that strain the eyes. Now, words on the screen have almost the same clarity as words printed on paper.

2007: Online book retailer Amazon.com releases the Kindle, made exclusively for the American market. The first lot of Kindles sells out in five and a half hours.

2008: Books on Board (booksonboard.com) starts selling eBooks for iPhones, the first online eBook store to do so.

August 2009: Sony links with libraries via the Overdrive digital network to enable people to borrow eBooks from libraries. Among the countries that have eBook borrowing are the United States and Singapore (no, Malaysia doesn't have it).

October 2009: Amazon.com releases Kindle 2, and ships it to more than 100 countries (no, Malaysia is not among them). In this month also, Barnes & Noble releases its own eBook reader, Nook.

November 2009: Students of the private Canadian secondary school, Blyth Academy, are supplied with Sony Readers loaded with their textbooks. It is the first school in the world to do this.

December 2009: Five major publishers, Conde Nast, Hearst,

Meredith, News Corp and Time Inc, announce that they will join forces to develop a format and an online store to beat Amazon.com's stranglehold on the eBook market. And on Christmas day, eBooks outsell physical books on Amazon.com for the first time ever.

January 2010 : At the Consumers electronic show, many new e-readers from Asus, Sony, Plastic Logic, Samsung and more, drive a frenzy of attention to e-readers and ebooks.

April 2010 :The Apple iPad debuts, and the iBookstore sells half a million ebooks in less than a month. BENQ and True Digital Form a partnership in Asia, and create a new Bookstore, creating a true Ebook conglomerate arises in the east.

FE-ink is set to soon be unseated from its dominant place in ereader display types however. Last year a UK company developed a prototype of a device that uses drops of oil in its display instead of drops of E-ink. One result of this was a display that refreshed up to a hundred times faster. The other big threat is tablet devices like the iPad, which are perfectly great ereaders in their own right as well as being able to do a hundred other things - like play videos and place phone calls.

In just a couple of years, the colour ereader has come a very long way, and the mind boggles at what lies in store in the next two. True, paper-thin epaper?

But still, some 11 million Americans are expected to own at least one digital reading gadget by the end of September, or so predicts Forrester Research. Additionally, the Association of American Publishers estimates that e-book sales in the United States grew 183% in the first half of this year compared with the year-earlier period.

Lower prices and the availability of more book titles have helped increase sales, but anyone can buy a book — the real challenge is actually reading it. But surveys have shown that people are in fact reading, just not by the fireside. It's not that people have more time to read than before, it's that they have more opportunities to read via e-Reader or mobile device than before. Whether it's on the train, in a waiting room or yes, in a hot tub, as long as you have your smartphone or e-Reader handy, you have a book.

And it's not just access to e-Readers that has us reading again. It's the accessibility of interfaces that is making it easier. We can increase fonts size, highlight text and zoom in. Functionality alone, is reason enough for some to put down print in favour of eReaders.

This is Your Brain on an eReader

However, there are still skeptics or at least those who worry that while we may be reading more, we're not soaking in as much. According to Jonah Lehrer at Wired.com, though digital books make content easier and easier to see, "It could actually backfire with books." He worries that:

We will trade away understanding for perception. The words will shimmer on the screen, but the sentences will be quickly forgotten.

In his article The Future of Reading, he studies how reading the printed word in actual print makes our brain work, explaining that:

…the act of reading observes a gradient of awareness. Familiar sentences printed in Helvetica and rendered on lucid e-ink screens are read quickly and effortlessly. Meanwhile, unusual sentences with complex clauses and smudged ink tend to require more conscious effort, which leads to more activation in the dorsal pathway. All the extra work – the slight cognitive frisson of having to decipher the words – wakes us up.

His solution? A feature that makes reading a little more difficult so as to force us to slow down and contemplate the meaning of words. His wish may have already come true, in a way. According to usability expert, Jakob Nielsen, iPad readers were 6.2% slower and Kindle readers were 10.7% slower at reading compared to print readers. Though the slowness is likely the result of screen technology, at least it's a start.

Digital books are definitely influencing how, what and when we read. And even if you doubt the longevity of e-Readers, it's still nice to know that, for now, one's access to books is better than before.

One in Six Americans Now Use E-Reader with One in Six Likely to Purchase in Next Six Months
e-Reader users likely to both read and purchase more books than non-users

"NEW YORK, N.Y. – September 19, 2011 – The options keep changing and bookstores are starting to feel the pressure. One major chain closed its doors for good this month while some of the others have rolled out their own e-Reader devices and are upgrading them regularly. Even The New York Times has changed the way it looks at bestsellers. It used to be just fiction and non-fiction; now it's also print versus e-Reader. And this is for a good reason as one in six Americans (15%) uses an e-Reader device up from less than one in ten (8%) a year ago. Also, among those who do not have an e-Reader, one in six (15%) say they are likely to get an e-Reader device in the next six months.

These are some of the results of The Harris Poll of 2,183 adults surveyed online between July 11 and 18, 2011 by Harris Interactive.

While some may lament the introduction of the e-Reader as a death knell for books, the opposite is probably true. First, those who have e-Readers do, in fact, read more. Overall, 16% of Americans read between 11 and 20 books a year with one in five reading 21 or more books in a year (20%). But, among those who have an eReader, one-third read 11-20 books a year (32%) and over one-quarter read 21 or more books in an average year (27%).

E-Reader users are also more likely to buy books. One-third of Americans (32%) say they have not purchased any books in the past year compared to only 6% of e-Reader users who say the same. One in ten Americans purchased between 11 and 20 books (10%) or 21 or more books (9%) in the past year. Again, e-Reader users are more likely to have bought, or downloaded books, as 17% purchased between 11 and 20 and 17% purchased 21 or more books in the past year.

Change in reading habits

One of the criticisms of e-Readers is that people who have them may download more books than they would traditionally purchase, but read at the same levels. So far this criticism is not holding true at all. Half of both e-Reader users (50% and non-users (51%) say they read the same amount as they did six months ago. However, while one-quarter of non e-Reader users (24%) say they are reading less than they did before (compared to just 8% of e-Reader users), over one-third of e-Reader users (36%) say they are reading more compared to just 16% of non-users.

Favorite Genre

Regardless of how they are reading it, there are types of books people like to read. Among those who say they read at least one book in an average year, three-quarters say they read both fiction (76%) and non-fiction (76%) but certain types of books rise to the top in both categories. Among fiction categories, almost half of readers say they read mystery, thriller and crime books (47%), while one-quarter read science fiction (25%), literature (23%) and romance (23%). One in ten read graphic novels (10%) while 8% read "chick-lit" and 5% read Westerns. Among non-fiction categories, almost three in ten readers say they read biographies (29%) while one-quarter read history (27%) and religious and spirituality books (24%). Just under one in five readers (18%) read self-help books, while 13% read true crime, 12% read current affairs, 11% read political books and 10% read business books.

Sales of eBooks

Sales of eBooks

The growth of ebooks sales in the last three years is unbelievable and the unique factor in that , is its by product. The increase in ebooks sales increased the total number of the readers of books in the same time .

It is like a miracle , the ebooks came in the right time to sustain and reverse the trend in the number of the people reading books . So, because of ebooks , the sales of books ; as a whole ; increased and the number of the readers of books increased dramatically too !

Here is a general view of the growth of ebooks as it stands today .. As stated by statistics published at ebookcomments.com .

' If growth in ebooks patterns is about $1.25 Billion in ebook sales in 2011.

Market shares

Quantity market shares of e-book sales in US by Goldman Sachs at 2010
[49]

Sellers		Percent
Amazon		58.0%
Barnes & Noble		27.0%
Apple		9.0%
Others		6.0%

And goodread.com stated in their report about ebooks the following ..

' The number of people who are reading ebooks in 2011 went up 163% over last year, and 36% up over the 4 months prior to 2011. This kind of growth is exciting and disruptive, and signifies that the publishing industry, which hasn't really changed in hundreds of years, is changing rapidly right before our eyes.

We should note that the numbers in the graph are probably actually higher, as not all members pay close attention to the format they catalog, and the hardcover edition is often the default. The trend however, is pretty clear.

Our data may confirm Amazon's trend report, but there are a few caveats that are important to keep in mind before we start declaring print is dead. Book readers buy books in all kinds of places, not just on Amazon. Recent news shows that the major publishers are seeing about 20% of their sales from ebooks. Recent internal surveys we have run show that people are still buying plenty of books from local bookstores and borrowing lots of books from the library.

Let's look at the Amazon data versus Goodreads data from one other perspective. As you know, at Goodreads we are more concerned with what people are reading rather than what people are buying. As such, we analysed our database for the top read ebooks of 2011:

We decided to see if we could mine our own data and find a similar trend. After analysing 19 million books people have marked as finished on Goodreads over the past three years and the 22 thousand books members currently mark as as finished each day, we found some pretty explosive looking ebook growth '

And 'The Wall Street Journal ' is predicting a little over $1billion in US ebook sales in 2011 and $2.0 billion in 2012.

Book TWO

To know thy Kindle !

Basics … How to ?

Getting started in few minutes !

Getting started in few minutes !

1 - Use the 5-way controller to select Connect to Wi-Fi. A list of available Wi-Fi networks is displayed.
You can connect wirelessly through your home Wi-Fi network, or places that offer Wi-Fi access, such as a hotel or your favorite café. Your Kindle automatically detects nearby Wi-Fi networks that broadcast their network name.
Select "connect" next to the network you wish to join. If you see a lock icon next to "connect," you'll need enter the Wi-Fi network password to connect. Press the Keyboard button to use the onscreen keyboard. Use the symbol keyboard to enter any numbers or symbols, and uppercase keyboard for uppercase characters.
Learn more about using your Kindle's onscreen keyboard.
The password is the one used to set up your Wi-Fi network, not your Amazon account password. If you don't know this password, please contact the person who set up your Wi-Fi network.
Once you have successfully connected to a Wi-Fi network, your Kindle will automatically reconnect to it when it detects a signal from that network.

2 - After you've successfully connected your Kindle to a Wi-Fi network, Set Up Your Kindle will guide you to register your Kindle.

If you have an Amazon account: Enter the e-mail and password of your Amazon account. Select "submit" using the 5-way controller. Your name will appear as the Registered User when registration is complete.

If you do not have an Amazon account: Use the 5-way controller to select this option and follow the onscreen instructions to set up a new account.

Having trouble registering? Consult Amazon troubleshooting guide for help with common issues.

3 - To be able to purchase eBooks , you have to set Up 1-Click Payment , to purchase content in the Kindle Store with your Amazon 1-Click Payment Method. Go to Manage Your Kindle. Click the Kindle Payment Settings link on left side of the page. Click on "Edit" under Kindle 1-Click Payment to update your payment method, then follow the onscreen instructions. Click "Continue" to verify your changes

4 - Once you've connected your device wirelessly, registered your Kindle, and set up your 1-Click Payment Method, you can start shopping for Kindle books and more from the Kindle Store right from your device. With your Kindle connected wirelessly, press Menu and choose "Shop in Kindle Store" to start downloading Kindle books and other content. All Kindle purchases from the Kindle Store are automatically backed-up online at Amazon and available through your Archived Items on your Kindle or online at the Manage Your Kindle page. You can re download content wirelessly for free, anytime.

THEN ... You need to charge your Kindle
* * *

Kindle ships with a USB cable. You can charge your Kindle by connecting it to your computer via the USB cable, or by connecting it to a wall socket using the USB cable and a Kindle power adapter (sold separately). The light on your Kindle next to the power button will appear yellow when charging and change to green when Kindle is fully charged.Power adapters are available for several countries and can be added to your Kindle order at the time of purchase or bought separately. Please visit the Kindle Store to see the available options .

When using the USB cable to charge your Kindle via your computer, charging time will normally take two to three hours.

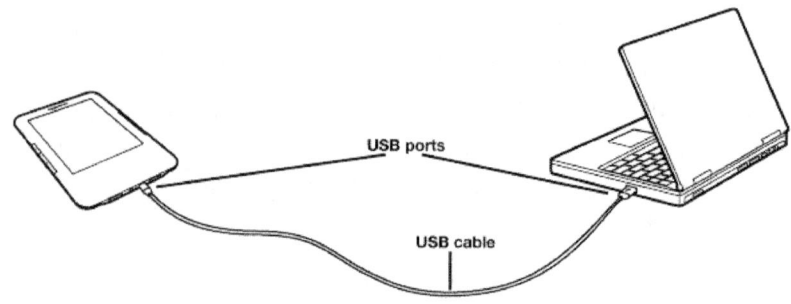

Now , the last thing to do is ' TO SET Your Kindle Clock '
To quickly check the time while reading, press Menu to display the time at the top of the screen. Once your Kindle has been registered, you can change the time on the clock:
From the Home screen, press the "Menu" button.
Select "Settings" and turn to the second page of Settings.
Use the 5-way controller to choose "set" or "set manually" next to the "Device Time."
Use the 5-way controller to adjust the hour, minutes, and a.m./p.m. settings.

Navigate to "save" and press to select.

What is a Kindle ?!

Kindle is a convenient, portable reading device with the ability to wirelessly download books, newspapers, magazines, and blogs. Books download in less than 60 seconds.

Designed to provide an exceptional reading experience, Kindle utilises a revolutionary new display technology called electronic paper. Reading Kindle's screen is as sharp and natural as reading ink on paper--and nothing like the strain and glare of a computer screen.

It is mobile and simple to use for everyone, and wireless. Kindle Keyboard allows you to connect your Kindle over a Wi-Fi network, and Kindle Keyboard 3G allows you the choice of connecting either via Free 3G or Wi-Fi.

Which Kindle ?!

As of today there are six different Kindles you can choose from at 11 different price-points. How ever will you decide? Here's a quick look at all of 'em, and our pre-release pick.

Kindle
Wi-Fi, 6" E Ink Display

The all-new Kindle - Lighter, smaller, faster
30% lighter, less than 6 ounces
18% smaller body, same 6" screen size - Fits in your pocket
Most advanced E Ink display, reads like paper
Built in Wi-Fi - Get books in 60 seconds
Massive book selection, over 800,000 titles are $9.99 or less
Borrow Kindle books from your public library

Kindle Touch
Wi-Fi, 6" E Ink Display

Kindle Touch 3G
Free 3G + Wi-Fi, 6" E Ink Display, 3G Works Globally

Simple-to-use touchscreen, with audio and built-in Wi-Fi
Most-advanced E Ink display, now with multi-touch
New sleek design - 8% lighter, 11% smaller, holds 3,000 books
Only e-reader with text-to-speech, audiobooks and mp3 support
Built in Wi-Fi - Get books in 60 seconds

Borrow Kindle books from your public library
Exclusive EasyReach touch technology lets you read easily with
one hand
New X-Ray feature lets you look up characters, historical figures,
and interesting phrases.

Kindle Keyboard, Wi-Fi, 6" E Ink Display

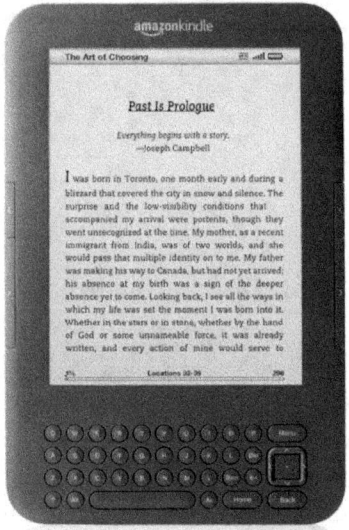

Lose Yourself in Your Reading
The most elegant feature of a physical book is that it disappears
while you're reading. Immersed in the author's world and ideas,
you don't notice a book's glue, the stitching, or ink. Our top design
objective is to make Kindle Keyboard disappear — just like a
physical book — so you can get lost in your reading, not the
technology.

Ergonomic Design

Kindle Keyboard is easy to hold and read. We designed our e-reader with long-form reading in mind. When reading for long periods of time, people naturally shift positions and often like to read with one hand. Kindle Keyboard's page-turning buttons are located on both sides, allowing you to read and turn pages from any position.

Simple Controls
Kindle Keyboard has an easy-to-use 5-way controller for on-screen navigation for highlighting text or looking up words. For searching and note-taking, Kindle Keyboard features a physical keyboard.

Never Gets Hot
Unlike a laptop, Kindle Keyboard never gets hot so you can read comfortably as long as you like.

Kindle Fire
Full Colour 7" Multi-touch Display, Wi-Fi

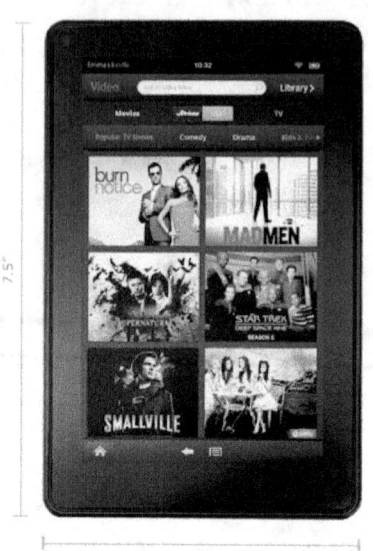

Movies, apps, games, music, reading and more, plus Amazon's revolutionary, cloud-accelerated web browser

18 million movies, TV shows, songs, magazines, and books

Thousands of popular apps and games

Ultra-fast web browsing - Amazon Silk

Free cloud storage for all your Amazon content

Vibrant colour touchscreen with extra-wide viewing angle

Fast, powerful dual-core processor

Amazon Prime members enjoy unlimited, instant streaming of over 10,000 popular movies and TV shows

To have the latest up-to-date information , and more details go to —

http://www.amazon.com/gp/product/B0051VVOB2/ref=famstripe_kf

Using the main controls

To get around on your Kindle Keyboard, you use the buttons, menus, and the keyboard.

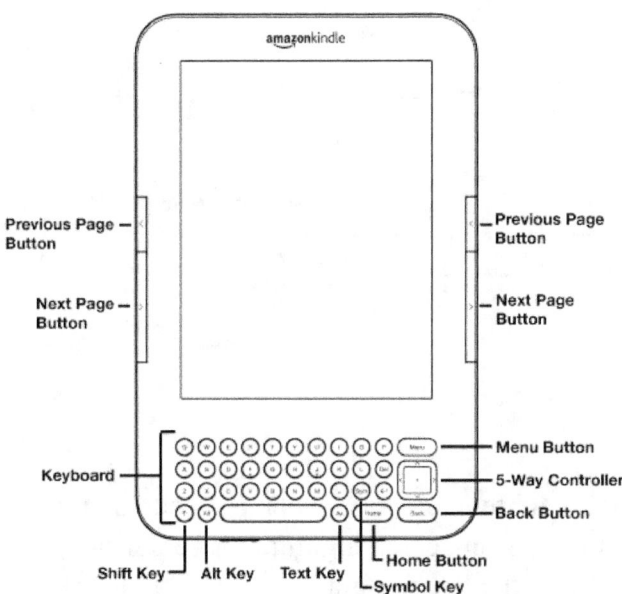

Volume controls: controls the headphone or speaker volume for audiobooks, background music, and Text-to-Speech.

* * *

"Previous Page" button: takes you to the previous page in your reading material.

"Home" button: shows content stored on your Kindle and directs you to your Archived Items.

"Next Page" button: takes you to the next page in your reading material. To accommodate different ways of holding the Kindle, there is a "Next Page" button on both sides.

"Menu" button: displays application and navigation choices that are related to the screen you are viewing.

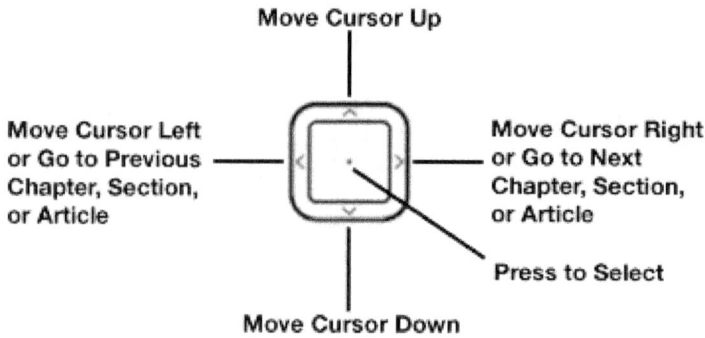

5-way controller: selects an item or action when pressed down. Use the arrows to control the on-screen highlight or cursor up,down, left, or right. Use the left or right arrows to skip to the next or previous chapter, section or article.

Keyboard: use to enter search terms, notes in your content, URLs for websites, etc.

* * *

"Back" button: retraces your steps on Kindle just like the "back" button on a web browser. For example, you can follow a link in a book and then press the "Back" button to return to your place. Symbol key: presents a menu of punctuation marks, numbers and symbols. Move the 5-way controller to select the desired symbol and press the 5-way to select.

Text key: changes the size of the text and number of words per line while you are reading and presents available controls for Text-to-Speech. Move the 5-way controller to select the optimal text size, words per line or a Text-to-Speech action.

Back View

The back of your Kindle contains stereo speakers for audio content.

BottomView

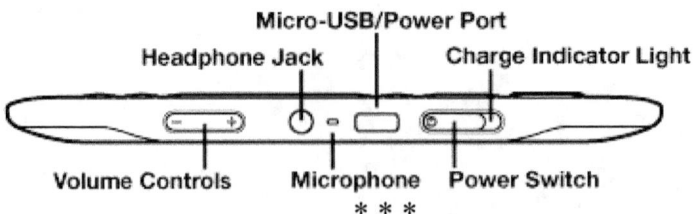

* * *

Power switch: puts your Kindle to sleep, wakes it up, and turns your Kindle on or off. To put your Kindle to sleep, slide and release the power switch; a full screen image appears on the display. While your Kindle is asleep, other keys and buttons are locked so that you don't accidentally change the place in your reading. To turn your Kindle off, slide and hold the power switch for seven seconds until the screen goes blank and then release. To wake up or turn on your Kindle, slide and release the power switch again.

If your Kindle does not power on or is unresponsive during use, try resetting the device by disconnecting your Kindle from any power source, and then sliding and holding the power switch for 15 seconds before releasing.

Tip: Your Kindle will also go to sleep by itself after 10 minutes if you are not using it. If your Kindle had wireless on prior to going to sleep, it will continue to receive your regularly scheduled subscriptions while in sleep.

Headphone jack: Plug in headphones to listen to an audiobook, background music, or content read aloud through Text-to-Speech. Attaching headphones turns off the built-in speakers.

Microphone: Kindle Keyboard is built with a microphone jack. This feature is not yet enabled and is for future use.

Micro-USB/power port: Attach the USB cord that came with your Kindle into the micro-USB/power port and into the Kindle power adapter. Plug the adapter into a U.S.-compatible electrical outlet to charge the Kindle battery. You can also charge your Kindle by detaching the USB cord from the power adapter and connecting it to a computer's USB port or powered USB hub. The charging status light will turn yellow, indicating that the battery is charging; you can continue to use your Kindle while it charges. A green light indicates that the battery is fully charged.

Check to make sure the power adapter is not covered by anything that could cause it to overheat. If the charge indicator light does not light up, make sure that the USB cable is fully inserted into your Kindle and the power adapter or USB port. If Kindle still is not charging, try another electrical outlet or USB port.

To transfer content between your computer and your Kindle, connect the provided USB cable to the Kindle and to the computer's USB port.

Content on Home Screen

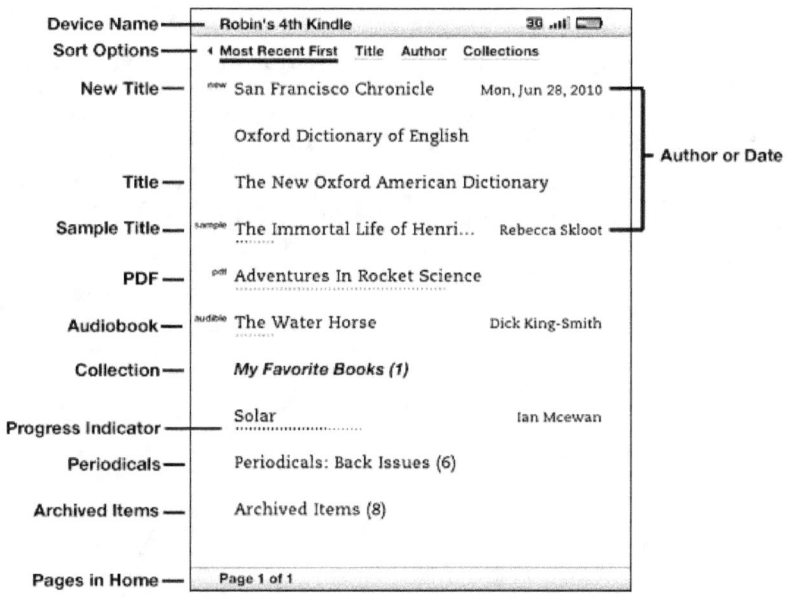

Kindle books: Books are shown by title and author, as well as any collections you have set up. Below the book title are a series of dots which give you an approximation of how long the book is. Bold dots within the series indicate how far along you are in the book based on the last page you viewed.

Periodicals: Periodicals include newspapers and magazines that can be purchased as a single issue or as a subscription delivered on a regular basis. Your Home screen lists the most recent issue of each periodical you have on your Kindle. Older issues are listed in "Periodicals: Back Issues" on your Kindle.

• Blogs: Subscription-based that appears on the Home screen as a single entry like books. Depending on the size and frequency of the entries, approximately 10 to 20 recent blog entries are available on your Kindle, and older entries are rolled off.

• Audiobooks: Audiobooks look similar to books, but they will be labeled in the Home screen as audio content. Like regular books, they have a progress indicator that shows where you are in the audiobook.

• Personal documents: Any personal documents such as text files or Digital Rights Management (DRM)-free e-books will appear on the Home screen under the title of the file that you transferred to Kindle.

Using the Menus

In addition to the physical buttons, you also navigate your Kindle Keyboard using the menus. Kindle's menus are context sensitive, but they all work the same way.

Use the 5-way controller to navigate within the menu and press the 5-way to select an item.
The illustration below shows the Home menu; the bold line under "Shop in Kindle Store" indicates that it is ready to be selected.

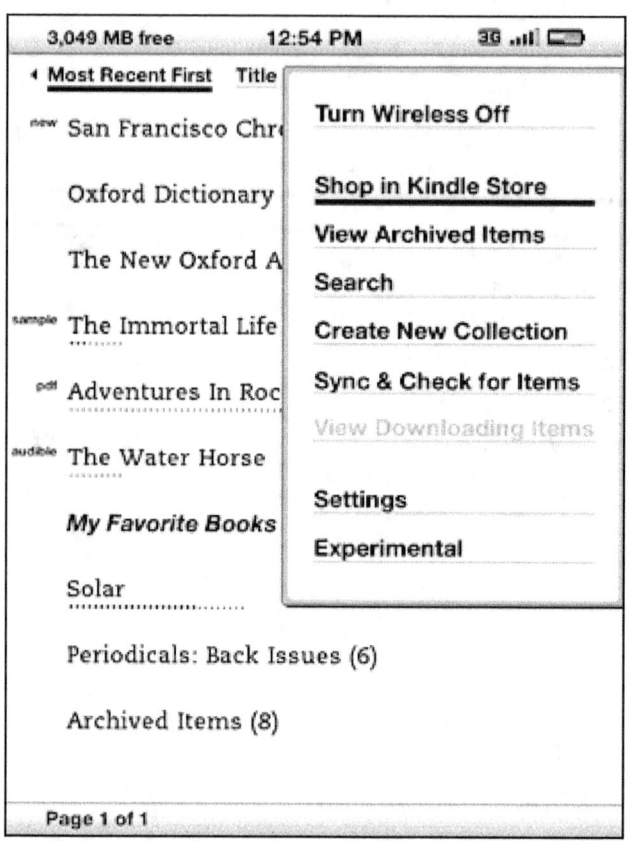

You can display a menu from any screen on your Kindle. When you press the Menu button, it displays choices related to the screen you are viewing. The sample screen below shows you the screen you would typically see when you press the Menu button from within a book.

Solar	10:44 AM	3G ..ıl 🔋

middle-class wom | **Turn Wireless Off**
abandon the cake :
child for such a
known he was bo | **Shop in Kindle Store**
claimed to have alv
scholarship to Oxfo | **Go to...**
for the rest of her l
same commitment | **Sync to Furthest Page Read**
bottle, sending her
her illness, on a C | **Book Description**
that she might try r
visits home. Her | **Search This Book**
meat-and-two-veg
the smell of olive | **Add a Bookmark**
reasons that rema
love from him. Sh | **Add a Note or Highlight**
legacy was clear: a
the attentions of be | **View My Notes & Marks**
Henry Beard wa | **View Popular Highlights**
mustache and sli
dark suits and br

large, especially around the neck. He provided for
his miniature family well and, in the fashion of the
time, loved his son sternly and with little physical

| 66% | Locations 2686-94 | 4337 |

Setting Up Wireless on Your Kindle

Kindle uses either Free 3G or Wi-Fi technology to enable you to wirelessly shop for and download Kindle content on the go. Your books are delivered wirelessly, typically in less than 60 seconds. If your Kindle has Wi-Fi and 3G, you can choose the most convenient wireless connection.

While you're reading, and for many other activities, your Kindle does not need to connect to a wireless network. Other activities such as shopping in the Kindle Store and purchasing books do require a wireless connection.

No monthly wireless bills, data plans, or commitments
Amazon pays for Kindle's wireless connectivity so you won't see a wireless bill. There is no wireless setup--you are ready to shop, purchase and read right out of the box.

See Wireless Terms and Conditions for your Kindle for more information.

Connecting wirelessly via Free 3G

For Kindle models that include Free 3G, wireless connectivity is automatic, so if you see one of the 3G network indicators (3G, EDGE, or GPRS) in the upper right corner of your Kindle screen, your Kindle is already connected wirelessly using 3G. Your Kindle automatically turns 3G coverage off when you connect using Wi-

Fi. If you disconnect from a Wi-Fi network or if you move out of Wi-Fi range, Kindle automatically switches back to 3G coverage. If you want to turn off 3G coverage, you can turn wireless off. Keep in mind that turning wireless off also disables Wi-Fi connections.

Learn more about Free 3G coverage.

Connecting wirelessly via Wi-Fi

If your Kindle uses Wi-Fi to connect wirelessly, you'll need to set up your Wi-Fi network.

Even if your Kindle has 3G, connecting via Wi-Fi will help you download content more quickly.

Tip: To check if you have a Wi-Fi only device or a Free 3G + Wi-Fi capable device, from the Home screen, press Menu, and use the 5-way controller to select "Settings." Under the "Device Info" section on the Settings page, see "Network Capability."

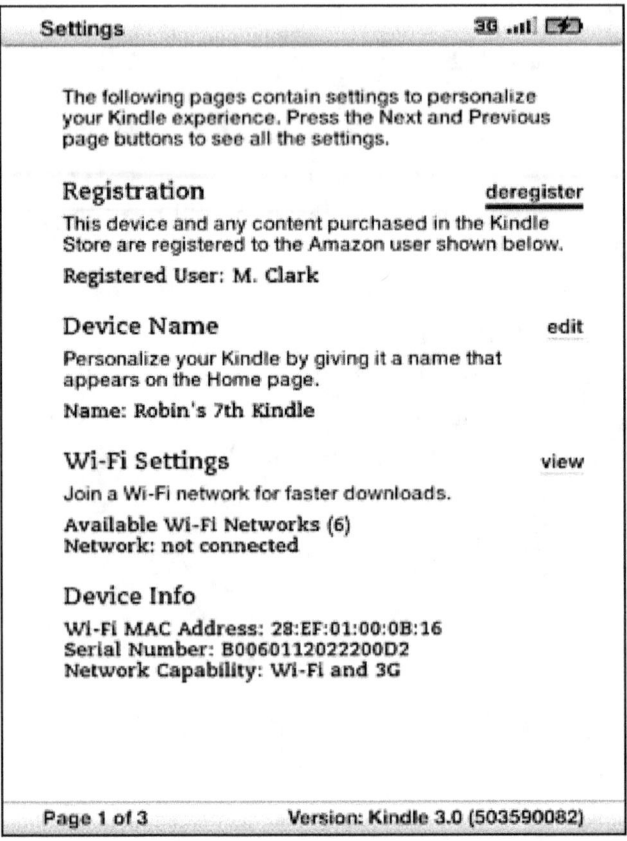

Setting Up Your Wi-Fi Network

You can connect wirelessly through your home Wi-Fi network, or public Wi-Fi hotspots, such as a hotel or your favorite café. Your Kindle automatically detects nearby Wi-Fi networks that broadcast their network name.

Learn how to connect to Wi-Fi in four easy steps, and troubleshoot common problems.

All AT&T hotspots across the U.S. also offer free Wi-Fi access for Kindle users (see a map of all AT&T hotspots.)

Public Wi-Fi hotspots usually don't require a password. Private Wi-Fi networks are usually password protected. Learn more about Wi-Fi password troubleshooting.

Connecting Your Kindle Wirelessly Video

Watch this video to learn how to wirelessly connect your Kindle via Wi-Fi.

Connecting with Wi-Fi

Your Kindle can connect to Wi-Fi networks or hotspots that use the 802.11b, 802.11g, or 802.11n (in B or G compatibility mode) standard. Kindle does not connect to enterprise or ad-hoc Wi-Fi networks (networks that allow peer-to-peer connections without a wireless access point). Keep in mind that you must be within range of one or more Wi-Fi networks in order to connect to one.

Manually Adding a New Wi-Fi Network

1.   Press the Home button, then press the Menu button.

2.   Navigate to "Settings" by moving the 5-way controller down, then press the 5-way controller to select.

3.   Select "view" next to "Wi-Fi Settings" to display a list of detected Wi-Fi networks. You may have to wait a moment as your Kindle detects networks in range. Kindle automatically scans for available Wi-Fi networks at periodic intervals. To rescan for available networks at any time, select "rescan."

4.   Select "connect" to connect to a network. If you see a lock symbol next to "connect," the network requires a password to connect.

5.   If necessary, enter the Wi-Fi network password, and choose "submit." Press the Symbol key to enter numbers or characters not present on the Kindle keyboard.

Once you are connected to a Wi-Fi network, Kindle automatically connects to it again whenever that network is in range. If more than one previously used network is in range, your Kindle automatically connects to the network that was most recently used. If your Kindle fails to connect to the new Wi-Fi network, it will display an "unable to connect" message. You can try manually entering all the network information for the Wi-Fi network by choosing "set up network" when you see the "unable to connect" message. If you don't know the network information, try connecting to a different network, or contact the network's administrator.

Tip: Once your Kindle connects to a Wi-Fi network, that network displays "forget" next to it in the list of available networks. Selecting "forget" disconnects your Kindle from that Wi-Fi network and also prevents Kindle from automatically connecting to it in the future.

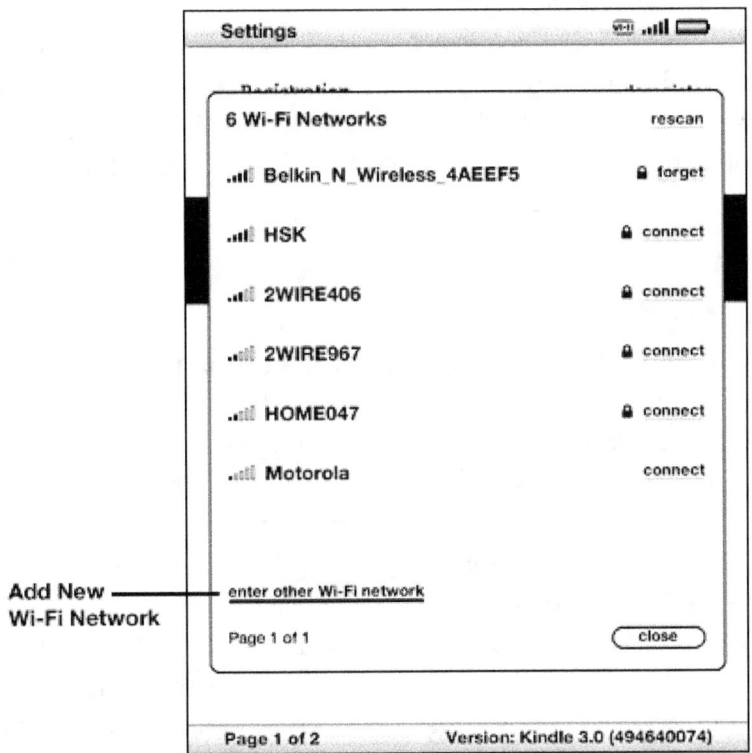

Add New Wi-Fi Network — enter other Wi-Fi network

Remembering and Forgetting Wi-Fi Networks

After you have successfully connected to a Wi-Fi network once, your Kindle will automatically connect to it again when it detects a signal from that network.
You can tell Kindle to forget a Wi-Fi network so that your Kindle doesn't connect to it automatically in the future.

    1.   While connected to the network that you want to forget, press the Home button, then press the Menu button.

    2.   Navigate to "Settings" by moving the 5-way controller

down, then press the 5-way controller to select.

3.   Select "view" next to "Wi-Fi Settings" to display a list of detected Wi-Fi networks. You may have to wait a moment as your Kindle detects networks in range. The Wi-Fi network you are currently connected to displays the word "forget" next to it in the list of available networks.

4.   Choose "forget" to disconnect from the network.

Tip: You can also download and transfer Kindle content from your computer to your Kindle via USB connection.

Free 3G Coverage Map

Kindle 3G (Free 3G + Wi-Fi) comes with built-in Free 3G wireless connectivity with coverage in more than 100 countries and territories. Check the 3G coverage in your area.

Kindle users living outside the United States

If you live outside the United States and use Kindle, please see Using Kindle if You Live Outside the United States.

Important information about the coverage map

The map may include areas served by unaffiliated carriers, and may depict their licensed area rather than an approximation of their coverage. Actual coverage area may differ substantially from map graphics, and coverage may be affected by such things as terrain, weather, foliage, buildings and other construction, signal strength and other factors. Amazon does not guarantee coverage.

Note: Please carefully review the Wireless Terms and Conditions for your Kindle, which explains the limitations of your service. Service is not available at all times in all places.

Syncing Material Across Your Devices

If you read the same Kindle Store book across multiple Kindles, you'll find Whispersync makes it easy for you to switch back and forth between devices and free Kindle reading applications. Whispersync synchronises the bookmarks and furthest page read among devices registered to the same account. Whispersync is on by default to ensure a seamless reading experience for a book read across multiple Kindles and Kindle apps.

To turn Whispersync off:

1.   Visit the Manage Your Kindle page.

2.   Click Manage Your Devices under Your Kindle Account on the left side of the page.

3.   Under Whispersync Device Synchronisation at the bottom of the page, click "Turn Off."

Once you turn Whispersync off, your books will still open to the last page read on that device, but Whispersync will no longer sync bookmarks or the furthest page read with other devices or apps. If you would like to sync the book manually on your device, press the Menu button and select "Sync to Furthest Page Read."

Receiving Your Kindle Content Wirelessly

All items currently available on your Kindle are displayed on your Home screen. To access additional Kindle content from your Kindle library, you can download content from your Archived Items folder or from the Manage Your Kindle page.

To download Archived Items wirelessly on your Kindle:

1.   Press the Menu button and select Turn on Wireless.

2.   Select "Archived Items" from the Home screen or press Menu and select "View Archived Items."

3.   Select the item from the Archived Items screen.

To send Archived Items wirelessly from Manage Your Kindle:

1.   Visit the Manage Your Kindle page.

2.   Locate the item you wish to download from Your Kindle Library. Use the View options at the top of the screen to narrow your results by displaying only books, newspapers, magazines, blogs, audiobooks, active content or loaned content.

3.   From the Actions drop down menu, click on "Deliver

to my..." and choose your Kindle or Kindle app from the list.

Wireless Status Indicators
The wireless status indicator in the upper right corner of your Kindle's screen shows whether wireless is turned on or off, the signal strength of your wireless service, and the connection speed. Here are the indicators and their meanings:

The wireless service is active and your Kindle has a strong signal. The more bars that are filled in with black, the stronger the wireless signal.

The bars are outlined in gray. This means wireless is checking for signal strength. This usually lasts less than 30 seconds.

OFF
The wireless service is turned off. You can turn on the wireless by pressing the Menu button, and using the 5-way controller to navigate to "Turn Wireless On."

Buying Content

The Kindle Store uses 1-Click Ordering and accepts most major credit and debit cards. You can view a list of payment methods we accept on the Paying by Credit Card and Check Card Help page. All prices are listed in U.S. Dollars (USD). To view or change the current payment method associated with your Kindle, please visit Manage Your Kindle on Amazon.com.

Downloading New Content

If you just purchased content from the Kindle Store or are waiting for the most recent issue of a periodical to be delivered, you can use Kindle's Home menu to start the download.

To download content pending delivery:

    1.   If you are not already on the Home screen, press the Home key.

    2.   Check the wireless status indicator to make sure you are connected to wireless. If not, select "Turn Wireless On" from the Home menu.

    3.   Press the Menu button and select "Sync & Check for Items" using the 5-way controller.

If you use lose your wireless connection while downloading, the download will resume once you regain your wireless connection.

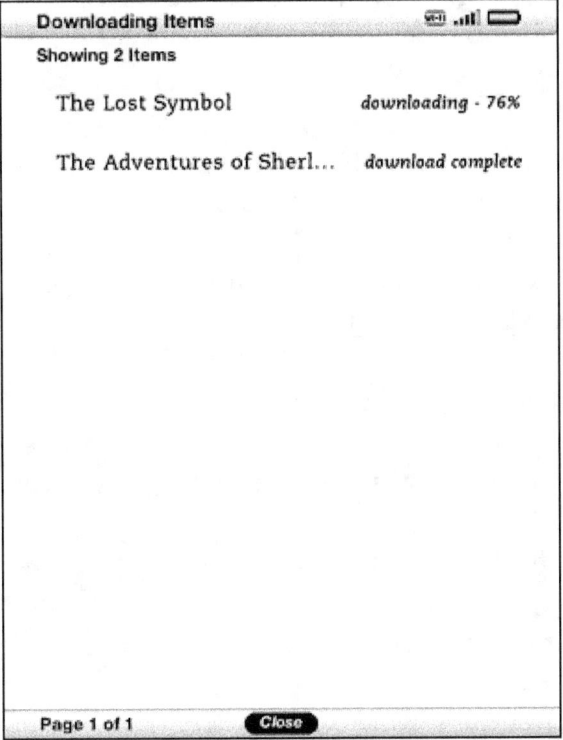

Removing kindle Content

All books you purchase are automatically backed up on Amazon.com. When you remove a book from your Kindle, it appears in your Archived Items.
To permanently remove a book so that it will no longer appear in your Archived Items, See Managing Your Kindle on Amazon.com. To remove content:

    1.   If you are not already on the Home screen, press the "Home" button.

    2.   Underline the item you want to remove with the 5-way controller.

    3.   Move the controller to the left and select "Remove from device."

To change your mind, move the 5-way up or down to cancel.

Removing Personal Content

Personal documents you transfer to your Kindle via your [name]@kindle.com e-mail address are backed up in your Kindle Library if the AutoArchive settings have been selected in Manage Your Kindle. The default setting is activated. If you transferred your personal document via USB or your AutoArchive settings were not activated when you transferred the personal document wirelessly, and you wish to keep a backup copy, you'll need to save them to your computer or another storage device before deleting them from your Kindle.

Removing Content with Annotations

When you remove a Kindle book you bought from Amazon that is available for re-download in your Kindle Library, we automatically save all of your annotations for the book.

The "My Clippings" file on your Kindle will still remain as a separate file containing all the clippings you added regardless of whether the content is a book, subscription, or blog, regardless of whether it was purchased from Amazon or not. See Customize Your Reading for more information.

Downloading Archived Content

Kindle displays the items you've downloaded on the Home screen. If you have Kindle content stored in your Kindle Library that isn't displayed, you can download it from your Kindle Library on Amazon.com when connected to wireless.

To download Archived Items:

     1.   Select "Archived Items" from the Home screen or press the Menu button and select "View Archived Items."

     2.   Select the item from the Archived Items screen.

More control … How to ?

Using The Dictionary

While reading a book or periodical, you can see a brief definition of a word using the built-in dictionary. By default, the built-in dictionary uses

The New Oxford American Dictionary.

To see the definition of a word in your reading:

    1.   Move the 5-way controller up or down to display and place the cursor in front of the word.

    2.   If the word is found in the dictionary, a definition extract appears at the bottom of the screen.

    3.   To see the complete definition, press the Return key. Use the Previous Page and Next Page buttons to view other word definitions.

    4.   Press the Back button to return to your reading.

Choosing your primary dictionary

You can choose the dictionary you want to use when you look up words while you are reading. The default is The New Oxford American Dictionary included on your Kindle, but Kindle Keyboard also comes with The

Oxford Dictionary of English. You can purchase additional supported dictionaries in the Kindle Store. To change your default dictionary:

    1.   If you are not already on the Home screen, press the

"Home" button.

    2.   Press the Menu button.

    3.   Move the 5-way controller to underline "Settings" and press to select.

    4.   Press the Menu button.

    5.   Move the 5-way to underline "Change Primary Dictionary" and press to select.

    6.   Move the 5-way to underline the dictionary you want to use and press to select.

Setting Text Size ,and More !

You can choose from eight different font sizes and several font styles to choose a style you can read comfortably. The text size of menus and other screens is fixed and cannot be modified. Kindle also allows you to change your screen rotation and set your preferred line spacing and words per line.

look at the universe with two eyes, and it is okay, fine. You have become a fully decent human being for the first time, but you do not have to proclaim that. You stop at red lights. You drive when it is green. It's a boring world. One has to take the first step. Then you find that you still maintain the same old standing, which is sometimes terrible, sometimes good, but still standing steady. It is

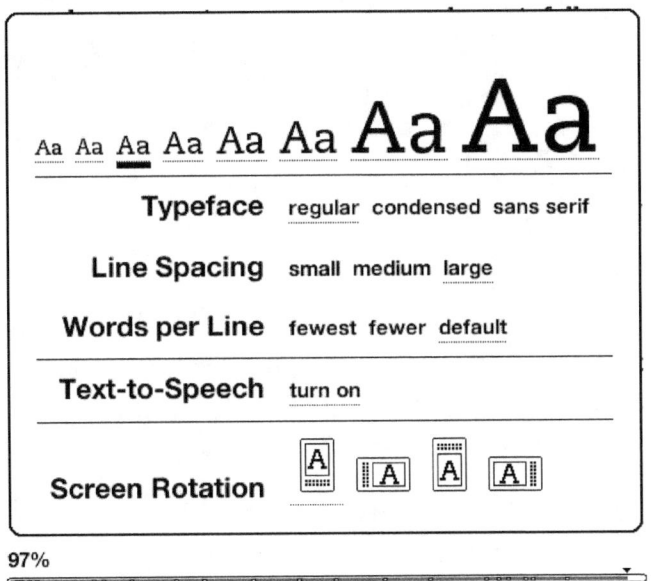

97%

To change your text formatting options:

1.   Press the Text key on the keyboard to display the

text size menu.

    2.   Select the desired text size, words per line, or screen rotation.

Navigatiog While Reading !

Press the Menu button when reading a book or periodical to display menu options that will help you navigate your Kindle content. You will have slightly different options depending on the type of content you are reading.

If you are reading a Kindle book, the menu shows the following options:

Turn Wireless Off: turns off wireless. When wireless is off, this option will change to "Turn Wireless On."

Shop in Kindle Store: takes you to the Kindle Store.

Go to ... : enter a specific location or page number to jump to that part of your book. You'll need to push the SYM key to enter the page number or location, and press SYM again to close the symbols screen. Use the 5-way controller to highlight and select the location button or the page button. If page numbers aren't available in the book you are reading, you won't be able to select the page button. You can also use the 5-way controller to navigate to the cover, beginning, end or contents of the book.

Sync to Furthest Page Read: connects to Amazon.com and compares your current reading location with the one saved at Amazon. If you are further along in your book using another device, Kindle gives you the choice to go to the furthest page read.

Book Description: connects to the Kindle Store and displays the detail page for the full book.

Search This Book: displays the search line at the bottom of the screen. Enter text to begin searching for a particular term or phrase within the book.

Add a Bookmark: bookmarks the page you are currently on. After selecting this option, the upper right corner of the book will be dog-eared and this menu option will change to "Delete Bookmark."

Add a Note or Highlight: puts you into annotation mode. Additional details on how to create a note or highlight are provided later in this chapter.

View Notes & Marks: displays a page containing all of your current item's notes, highlights, bookmarks, and clippings.

View Popular Highlights: displays a list of the most Popular Highlights from Kindle users.
Jumping to the Next or Previous Chapter: You can use the Kindle 5-way controller to skip to the next or previous chapter within many books. Simply press the 5-way controller to the right to skip forward a chapter or left to skip back a chapter.
Note: Not all Kindle content is enabled to jump from chapter to chapter. Books that have this feature enabled will display chapter breaks as small dots within the progress bar at the bottom of the screen.

1%

If you are reading a periodical or blog, you will see the following different options:

Clip This Article: makes a copy of the entire article and adds it to your "My Clippings" file.

Keep This Issue: designates the newspaper or magazine issue as one to be stored in your Kindle until you remove it.

Seeing Page Locations and Numbers

As you read, you'll see your progress displayed at the bottom the screen as a percentage of the Progress Indicator.

reason—to study Italian just because they feel like it. Not one of us can identify a single practical reason for being here. Nobody's boss has said to anyone, "It is vital that you learn to speak Italian in order for us to conduct our business overseas." Everybody, even the uptight German engineer, shares what I thought was my own personal motive: we all want to speak Italian because we love the way it makes us feel. A sad-faced Russian woman tells us she's treating herself to Italian lessons because "I think I deserve something beautiful." The German engineer says, "I want Italian because I love the *dolce vita*"—the sweet life. (Only, in his stiff Germanic accent, it ends up sounding like he said he loved "the *deutsche vita*"—the German life—which I'm afraid he's already had plenty of.)

As I will find out over the next few months,

15%

Page Numbers

Kindle's page numbers match the page numbers in print books so you can easily reference and cite passages, and read alongside others in a book club or class.

If your Kindle book includes page numbers, you'll see page numbers displayed next to locations when you push the Menu button. Page numbers and locations are only displayed when the Menu button is pushed.

Not all Kindle books include page numbers. Kindle books that include page numbers will list "Page Numbers Source ISBN (the print book identification number)" for the matching print edition under "Product Details" on the detail page at Amazon.com. If the Page Numbers Source ISBN (the print book identification number)" listed under "Product Details" on the product detail page is the same edition as your print book, the Kindle page numbers will match the page numbers in the printed edition.

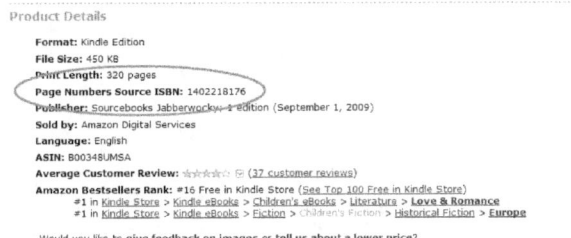

Because Kindle books allow you to change font size and other features, you may be able to view more than one page on your screen at once. Only the corresponding page number for the text displayed at the top left of the screen will be shown.

Page numbers are only displayed on Kindle Keyboard with software version 3.1 or higher. To update your Kindle's software, visit www.amazon.com/kindlesoftwareupdates.

Locations

Kindle books also mark your progress using locations. Location numbers are specific to each line of text so you can easily find a particular passage, regardless of changes you may make to text size.

Press Menu to display the location information at the bottom of the screen above the Progress Indicator.

Chapter, Section, and Article Breaks

If the book you are reading shows chapter, section or article breaks, displayed as breaks as small dots within the progress bar, you can jump between these using the 5-way controller.

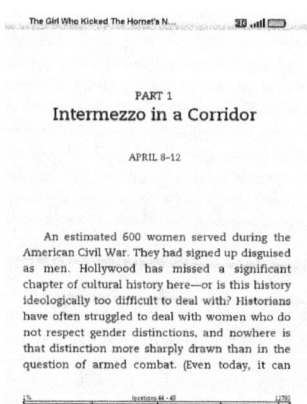

While reading, move the controller to the left or right to skip ahead to the next chapter or return to the previous chapter. This feature will also allow you to skip from one section to another or one article to another.

Searching on Kindle !

Kindle's search function allows you to find related items in your content and on the Internet.
To perform a search:

    1.   Type in your search term, the Search line will automatically appear. You can use whole words or partial words, and no distinction is made between lower and upper case. You can enter up to 255 characters.

    2.   Move the 5-way to the right to highlight the content or location to search and press the 5-way to select. The arrow indicates that more Search options are available if you scroll in the direction indicated.

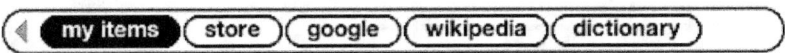

Types of Searches
Here's a quick description of the available search options:

    •   Find: Searches the item you're currently reading for the search term(s).

    •   My Items: Searches all of your content (including text, metadata and annotations in downloaded items, archived items, personal documents, and local reference materials) for the search term(s).

- Store: Searches for your term(s) in the titles, descriptions, and content of items available for purchase from the Kindle Store.
- Google: Searches Google.com for indexed websites containing the search term(s).
- Wikipedia: Searches Wikipedia.com for entries containing the search term(s).
- Dictionary: Searches your default dictionary on your Kindle for the search term(s).

Viewing Search Results

Kindle displays a Search Results page when the requested search is completed. Use the Next Page and Previous Page buttons if there are more results than fit on the current page. If your results contain a specific item or website, you'll be able to underline and select specific items using the 5-way controller.

My Items

Kindle displays all titles that contain your search term(s) and shows total instances for your term(s) in each item to the left of the title. To see all results for a specific title, select it with the 5-way controller.

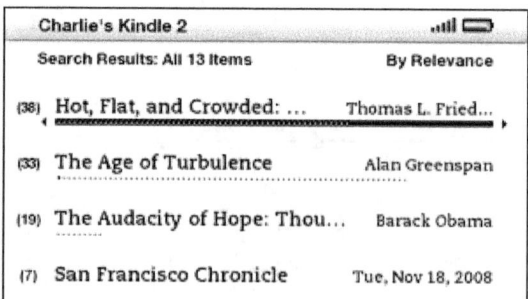

After you select a specific title from the search results or if you limited your search results to a specific title originally, you'll see a results page that displays all the locations where the search term(s)

appear. You can select and view the locations listed using the 5-way controller. Use the Back button to return to your results page.

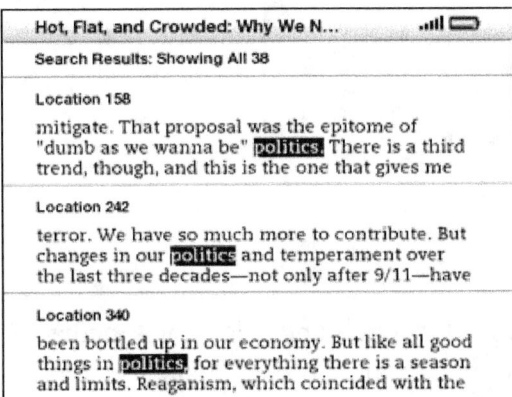

Kindle Store
A Store search takes you to the Kindle Store where you can browse available titles.

Definitions
When you look up the meaning of a word, Kindle displays definitions from default dictionary. You can use the 5-way controller to select specific words within the definition to see them

defined at the bottom of the screen.

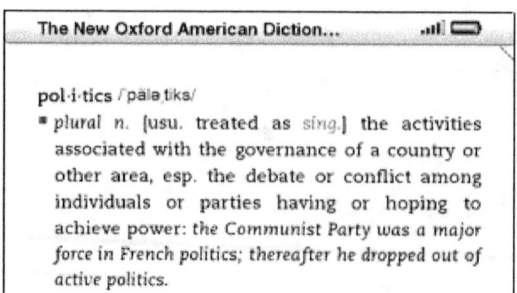

Remote Searches
When you're connected to Whispernet and select "wikipedia" or
"google" as your search option, Kindle opens Basic Web and
displays the search results from the chosen website. If links are
available, you can navigate to other web pages using the 5-way
controller.

Zooming on Images

If you'd like to zoom in on an image, Kindle gives you tools to set a custom size.

To zoom on an image in a book:

1. Position the cursor over the picture using the 5-way controller to make a magnifying glass icon appear.
2. Press the 5-way to zoom the image.
3. Press the 5-way to return to your content.

When Kindle increases the image size, your view may change from portrait or landscape if necessary to maximise the use of the display.

Sorting Content and Using Collections

Kindle allows you to choose how the content on the Home screen is sorted.

To change how your content is organised on the Home screen:

    1.   Move the 5-way controller up to the top of the screen to underline the current Sort setting. The default setting is "By Most Recent First."

    2.   Move the 5-way to the right to see the Sort options.

    3.   Select your desired option using the 5-way controller. Here's a list of the Sort options available:

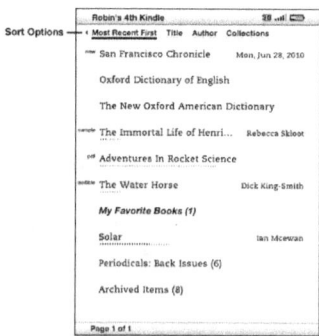

    •   Most Recent First: Sorts your content by the most recently added or recently opened items first.

    •   Title: Sorts your content alphabetically by title of the item.

    •   Author: Sorts your content alphabetically by the

author's last name or publisher's name. If you choose this option, periodicals will be sorted by their dates.

• Collections: Sorts content based on categories you create on your Kindle to organise your content.

Creating Collections

If you store a lot of content on your Kindle, you can create collections to improve your organisation. A collection is a category you create on your Kindle Home screen. You can then move your books, audiobooks, and personal documents from the Home screen to the collections you create. Your Kindle will sort your content by collections after you create your first collection.

Kindle Home without Collections

Content Organised into Collections

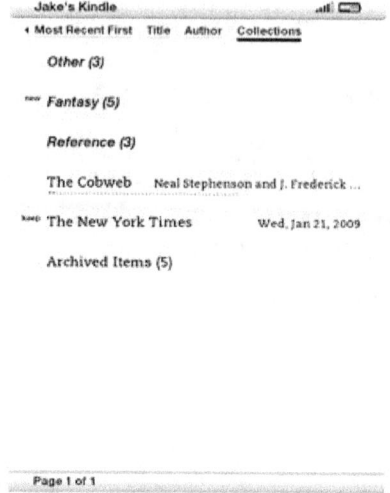

To create a collection:

1.   Select "Create New Collection" from the Home screen menu.

2.   Enter a name for the collection.

3.   Select "Save" with the 5-way controller when finished.

To rename or delete a collection:

1.   Highlight the collection name on the Home screen.

2.   Move the 5-way controller to the right to reveal the collection options.

3.   Select the desired action with the 5-way controller.

4.   Follow the on-screen instructions.

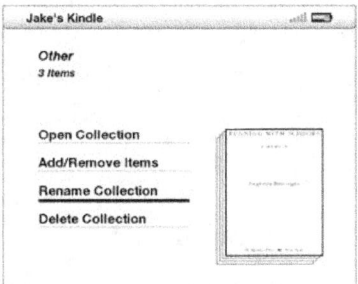

Note: Deleting a collection from your Kindle does not change the content stored on your device. Items previously placed into the collection that are stored on your Kindle will appear on the Home screen after the collection is deleted.

To sort your Home screen content by collection:

1.   Move your cursor to the top of the Home screen to highlight "Showing All Items" and your current viewing option.

2.   Move the 5-way controller to the right to reveal available viewing options.

3.   Select "Collections" from the options.

Managing Content in Your Collections

After you create one or more collections, you're ready to associate books, audiobooks, and personal documents on your Kindle using those collections. Please note that subscriptions such as newspapers, magazines, and blogs cannot currently be added to collections on the Kindle. Here are a few handy collection features:

•   Collections are stored on Amazon: When you create a collection on a device, we'll save your collection so it appears in Archived Items on other devices registered to your Amazon.com account. This allows you to transfer collections across registered Kindles.

• Kindle content is associated with a collection until removed: If you add a book or other content to a collection on your Kindle and then delete the book from your device, it remains associated with that collection in Archive Items. If you download the item again, it will automatically appear in the appropriate collection on your Home screen.

• Books and other content can appear in more than one collection: You can associate a single book or other item from your library with multiple collections if you wish.

• Collections don't change device or Archive Items content: If you delete Kindle content from a collection or delete an entire collection from your Kindle, it does not change the actual items saved on your Kindle or in your Archive Items on Amazon. When you delete a collection from your Kindle, any downloaded items from that collection will appear the Home screen instead of in the collection.

To add or remove collection items:

1. Highlight the collection name on the Home screen.
2. Move the 5-way controller to the right to reveal the collection options.
3. Select "Add/Remove Items" with the 5-way controller.
4. Highlight and select a title you wish to add or remove. Items currently in the collection will display a check mark to the right of the title.
5. Select "Done" at the bottom of the screen when you've finished editing your collection.

To import a collection from another Kindle:

1. Select "Archived Items" from the Kindle Home screen.
2. Select "Add Other Device Collections" from the Archived Items page.
3. Select the desired collection to import and select "OK"

to confirm.

Note: Importing a collection from another device does not import the books or other items to your Kindle if they aren't downloaded already. However, books already on your Kindle that are associated with a collection will automatically appear under that collection name on your Home screen.

What is Public Notes ?!!

Public Notes allow you to connect with fellow readers by seeing what passages they found meaningful in books you are both reading.

You can search for and follow other readers at https://kindle.amazon.com.

If someone you follow has highlighted a passage in a book and has turned on Public Notes for the book, you'll see that passage highlighted along with the name of the person who highlighted it. The"@" symbol will be displayed in the text where any notes were made.

Public Notes will also appear in a list with your personal annotations if you select "View Notes and Marks" from the menu while reading. By default, Public Notes are displayed in your books but you can turn them off if you don't want to see them.

To turn Public Notes on and off:

     1.   Navigate to Kindle's Home screen and press the Menu button.

     2.   Select "Settings."

     3.   Select the desired option next to "Public Notes."

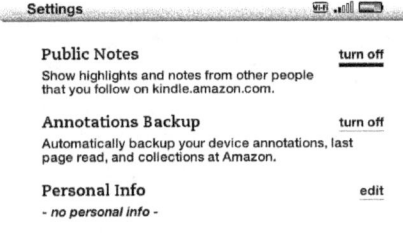

Turning Public Notes on or off from your device will not make your notes visible. You have to turn on Public Notes for a book through our website before anyone else can see your highlights and notes in that book. Go to https://kindle.amazon.com/ your_reading make your highlights and notes visible through Public Notes.

Following other readers to see their Public Notes

Authors, book club members, thought leaders, passionate readers, professors and all Kindle users can opt-in to sharing their notes with other readers.

To follow other readers:

1. Visit https://kindle.amazon.com
2. Log in using your Amazon account details.
3. Search for the name of the person you would like to follow in the search bar in the top right corner.
4. Click the "Follow" button. If you'd like to stop

following this person in the future, simply select the "Stop Following" button.

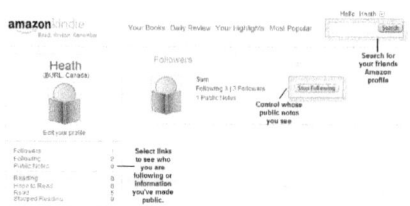

Sharing your Public Notes

1.   Visit kindle.amazon.com and select "Your Books" from the options on the top of the screen.

2.   Check the boxes to select what information you would like to share about any of your books.

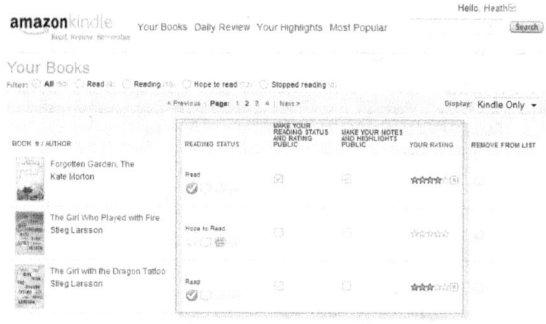

You can also make a single note a Public Note and share it with people following you by selecting "save & share." This will also post the highlighted passage and any comment you add to the social media networks you have associated with your Kindle account.

* * *

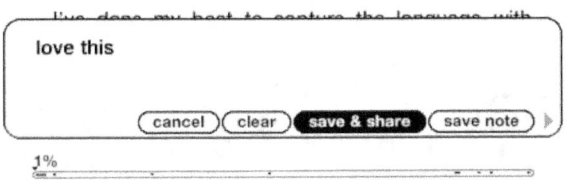

To share a single Public Note:
You can make any highlight or note a Public Note, without setting
Public Notes for that book online.

    1.   Place the cursor at the beginning of the passage using
the 5-way controller and press down to anchor it.

    2.   Highlight the passage using the 5-way controller.

    3.   Enter your note or comment about the passage you
highlighted. (There is a 100 character limit.)

    4.   Select "save & share" from the options at the bottom of
the note window when finished.

Only this single highlight or note will be shared with other readers
following you. You have to turn on Public Notes for the entire
book to make all your notes and highlights from that book public.
If you don't have a Facebook or Twitter account associated with
your Kindle account, you'll automatically be prompted to manage
your social network registration before your message is posted. If
you choose not to link your Kindle account to your social media
networks, your highlights and notes will still be saved in the book,
as well as at https://kindle.amazon.com.

Bookmarks , Clippings , Notes !

Information about using Kindle is also available in your Kindle User's Guide--you can download a copy on the Kindle Documentation page.

Overview of Annotations

Annotations (bookmarks, highlights, notes, clippings) you make on a Kindle book are stored in your Kindle Library on Amazon.com when your Kindle is connected to wireless. When you open the title on any registered device, you'll be right where you were the last time you read and your annotations will be included.

To view your annotations: Open your title, press the Menu button and select "My Notes & Marks."

Adding Bookmarks

You can place a bookmark at any location and place multiple bookmarks in whatever you are reading. Select "View Notes & Marks" to return to any bookmarked location. Bookmarked pages have a "dog-ear" icon in the upper right corner.

To place a bookmark:

    1.   Go to the page that you want to bookmark.

    2.   Press the Menu button.

    3.   Highlight and select "Add a Bookmark" using the 5-way controller.

Tip: You can quickly create a bookmark by either holding down the Alt key and pressing the B key, or by moving the 5-way up or down to go into cursor mode and then pressing the 5-way controller twice.

To view a bookmarked location:

1.   Press the Menu button and Select "My Notes & Marks."

2.   Highlight and select the desired location from the list.

To remove a bookmark:

1.   Go to the bookmarked page.

2.   Press the Menu button.

3.   Highlight and select "Delete Bookmark."

Highlighting Passages

You can highlight text in Kindle like you would use a highlighter pen on paper and view them at any time by pressing the Menu button and selecting "View Notes & Marks." The text you highlight appears with a gray underline.

To highlight one or more lines:

1.   Use the 5-way to position the cursor where you want to start highlighting.

2.   Press the 5-way to anchor the cursor.

3.   Move the 5-way to select the desired text. Use Next Page or Prev Pages to highlight text across multiple pages.

4.   Press the 5-way at the place where you want the highlight to end.

To remove a highlight:

1.   Press the Menu button and select "View Notes & Marks."

2.   Underline the highlight you want to remove with the 5-way controller.

3.   Press the Delete key.

4.   Repeat steps 2 and 3 to remove additional highlights.

5.   Select "Close Notes & Marks" when finished.

Viewing Popular Highlights

Amazon displays Popular Highlights by combining the highlights of all Kindle customers and identifying the passages with the most highlights. The resulting Popular Highlights help readers focus on passages that are meaningful to the greatest number of people. Some books don't have enough highlighting in them to have Popular Highlights. Popular Highlights are marked with a gray dashed underline. The number of people who have highlighted the text appears at the beginning of the marked text. You can see Popular Highlights for all books that have them at https:// kindle.amazon.com.

To view Popular Highlights:

1. Open a book on your Kindle.

2. Press the Menu button and select "View Popular Highlights" from the options.

To turn Popular Highlights on and off:

1. Navigate to Kindle's Home screen and press the Menu button.

2. Select "Settings."

3. Select the desired option next to "Popular Highlights."

Managing Popular Highlights

If you have a Kindle device, you can turn off having your highlights in popular highlights by turning off Annotations Backup in Settings on your device. If you have a Kindle App, we will be adding this capability soon. Annotations BackUp backs up your annotations and last page read and syncs them across devices. You can also remove highlights you made previously from Popular Highlights.

To turn off Annotations Backup:

1. Navigate to Kindle's Home screen and press the Menu button.

2. Select "Settings."

3. Select the desired option next to "Annotations

Backup."
To remove previous highlights from Popular Highlights:

    1.   Visit the <u>Amazon Kindle</u> website and log in using the e-mail address and password for the Amazon account you used to register your Kindle.

    2.   Select "Your Highlights" from the Browse options at the top of the page.

    3.   Select "Delete this highlight" next to each highlight you wish to remove.

Adding Notes

Kindle Keyboard allows you to add comments, make notes, and mark up passages just as you might in a printed book.
To add a note:

    1.   Move the cursor to where you want to place a note using the 5-way controller.

    2.   Type your note.

    3.   Select "save note" at the bottom of the screen.

A superscripted number appears where you inserted your note. Notes are numbered in the order they appear in the content and update automatically if you add more.
To edit or delete a note:

    1.   Select the note's number using the 5-way controller so the note appears at the bottom of the screen.

    2.   Press the Return key to edit the note or the Delete key to delete the note.

    3.   Use the keyboard to make changes if editing.

    4.   Select "save note" to save any changes.

Making Clippings

You can "clip" an entire periodical article and save it to the "My Clippings" file.
To clip an article:

    1.   Go to the article you want to clip.

    2.   Press the Menu button.

3.　　Select "Clip this Article."

To view your clippings:

1.　　Press the Home button to display the Home screen.

2.　　Select "My Clippings" from the Home screen.

Editing the "My Clippings" File

All of your bookmarks, highlights, notes, and clippings are stored in the "My Clippings" TXT file on your Kindle. You can transfer and copy the file to share and use your clippings.

To transfer the "My Clippings" file and open it on your computer:

1.　　Connect your Kindle to your computer using the USB cable.

2.　　Use your computer's file browser to view the Documents folder on Kindle.

3.　　Transfer the "My Clippings" file from Kindle to your computer.

4.　　Open the "My Clippings" file on your computer using an application that can read or import a .TXT file.

If you wish, you can make changes to the file and transfer it back to your Kindle. Changing your "My Clippings" file does not affect any notes, bookmarks, or highlights you've made in the actual content. The next time you read the content, you can still use them for navigation and reference.

To remove the "My Clippings" file from your Kindle:

1.　　Press the Home button to display the Home screen.

2.　　Underline "My Clippings" on the Home screen.

3.　　Move the 5-way controller to the left.

4.　　Press the 5-way to select "Delete."

Kindle adds a new "My Clippings" file the next time you add a clipping or annotation to any content.

Total control … How to ?

Talk to Me, My Kindle !

Voice Guide lets you navigate your Kindle Keyboard with spoken menus, selectable items, and descriptions. For example, when you open a book, Kindle Keyboard speaks your current location and how far you've read.

To turn Voice Guide on or off, follow these steps:

1. If you are not already on the Home screen, press the Home button.
2. Press the Menu button.
3. Move the 5-way to underline "Settings" and press to select.
4. Press Next Page to go to Page 2 of Settings.
5. Move the 5-way to underline "turn on" or "turn off" next to the "Voice Guide" setting and press to select.

If your Kindle Keyboard has software version 3.3 or higher you can quickly turn Voice Guide on and off by holding down the Shift key and pressing the Spacebar on your keyboard. If you don't have the latest software version on your Kindle Keyboard yet, download the latest version of Kindle software here.

Listening to Audiobooks !

Audible offers five versions of its audiobook format.

- Kindle is compatible with Audible audio format 4 and Audible Enhanced (AAX).
- Audiobooks provided from other sources are not supported.

Audible files appear on your Kindle Home screen with the word "audible" next to the title. You can purchase and download audiobooks from Audible.com and then transfer these books over USB or Wi-Fi to your Kindle's "Audible" folder.See Transferring, Downloading, and Sending Files to Kindle for information about transferring audiobooks to your Kindle.

To listen to an audiobook:

1. Select an audiobook from your Home screen.
2. Select the desired action with the 5-way controller to start, skip through, and stop playback.

Here's a list of the options you'll see for listening to your audiobooks:

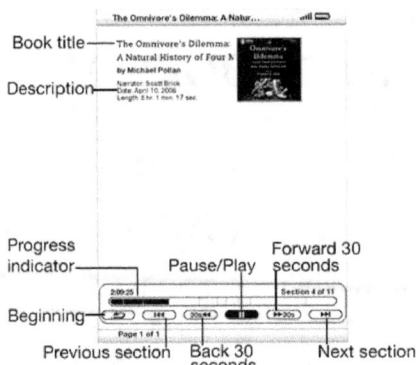

- Progress Indicator: indicates how far you have come in the audiobook, the elapsed time, and the section you are in.
- Pause/Play: pauses or plays the audiobook (there is no Stop control).
- Forward 30 Seconds: moves ahead thirty seconds from the current location.
- Beginning: takes you back to the beginning of the audiobook.
- Previous Section: moves backwards in the audiobook to the previous section.
- Back 30 Seconds: moves backwards thirty seconds from the current location.
- Next Section: moves ahead to the next section in the audiobook, which is usually the next chapter.

Tip: To pause the playing of Audible content, press the space bar on the keyboard and press the spacebar again to resume.

Activating Your Kindle with Audible.com

If you use Audible Download Manager or Audible Manager on your PC, your Kindle will automatically be activated. Mac users will be prompted to activate their Kindle with Audible.com the first time they transfer Audible.com audio content to their Kindle. If you have purchased Audible titles via the Kindle Store or linked your Amazon and Audible accounts via the Audible website, you can log in at Audible.com with your Amazon.com e-mail address and password. Otherwise, use your Audible.com username and password.

Requirements:

- Windows XP/Vista/Windows 7
- Audible Manager 5.5.0.3 or later
- Mac OS X (can be used to transfer content to Kindle

Transfering your music to your Kindle !

You can transfer your MP3 files to Kindle by copying them to the "music" folder on your Kindle over USB. For more information on connecting your computer over USB, see Transferring Files via USB.

Kindle only supports MP3 audio files; AAC, WAV and other music file formats are not supported.

To transfer MP3s to your Kindle, follow these steps:

1.

2.   Connect your Kindle to your computer, using the USB cable that came with the device.

3.

4.   Your Kindle should appear on your computer in the same location you would normally find an external USB drive.

5.

6.   Open your Kindle. You should see a folder entitled "music." Drag any MP3s you'd like to play on your Kindle into this folder.

7.

8.   Using your computer, un-mount your Kindle from your computer.

Tip: While there is no limit to the number of MP3 files and audiobooks that you can transfer to your Kindle, keep in mind that these files are larger, and space may become a consideration.

listen to Music While Reading !

You can transfer your favorite MP3 music files to your Kindle Keyboard using the USB connection and then listen to them while reading. You cannot play music when using Text-to-Speech or listening to an audiobook. See Listening to Music for more details.

Asking your Kindle to read to you !

Your Kindle can read aloud your books (where allowed by the rights holder), newspapers, magazines, blogs, and personal documents with the Kindle Experimental application, Text-to-Speech.

To turn on Text-to-Speech, follow these steps:

1.   Press the Text key **Aa** .

Aa	Aa	Aa	Aa	Aa	Aa

Words per Line	fewest fewer default
Text-to-Speech	turn on
Speech Rate	slower default faster
Speaking Voice	female male
Screen Rotation	[A] [A] [A] [A]

Move the 5-way down so that the "Text-to-Speech" option is underlined. Press the 5-way to select "turn on." In a few moments, you will hear your content spoken aloud. You can either listen to it through the Kindle's external speakers or plug in earphones into the headphone jack.

By default, content is spoken with a male voice, but

using the 5-way, you can select a female speaking voice. You can also slow down or increase the rate of speech as well as pause or turn off Text-to-Speech.

While Text-to-Speech is playing, the screen will update to the corresponding page of text.

For PDF files and books which the rights holder does not allow Text-to-Speech to read aloud their content, then "Text-to-Speech" will be grayed and you will not be able to select it.

By default, Text-to-Speech starts reading at the beginning of the page currently displayed. To start reading at a particular spot, move the cursor where you'd like the reading to begin before starting Text-to-Speech.

Tip: You can also play or stop Text-to-Speech by holding down the

Shift key and pressing the Symbol key . You can pause and resume Text-to-Speech by pressing the Spacebar.

… and Yes! Social Reading Too !

Finished reading a book
Now ! Share your opinion !
On the final page of a book, you can tweet/share that you've finished, rate the book, see recommendations for additional books and more books by this author.

View the final page at any time by selecting Menu, then "Go to," then "End."

Tweet/share via social media
Select "Tweet/share that you've finished this book" to let everyone know you've read it. You can enter or update a message before

sharing. A link to the book will also be appended to your message. If you don't have a Facebook or Twitter account associated with your Kindle account, you'll automatically be prompted to manage your social network registration before your message is posted.
To manage your social networks:

1. Navigate to Kindle's Home screen and press the Menu button.

2. Select "Settings."

3. Select the "manage" option next to Social Networks on the Settings page.

4. Follow the instructions on the screen to link or unlink an account.

Note: In order to share passages from your Kindle books through your social media networks, you must set the Country of Origin on the device. Go to Manage Your Kindle, scroll to Your Country and click Edit.

Rate This Book

Select "Rate this book." Select the number of stars you'd use to rate the book, then select "save & share."
You can rate the book at any time just by going to the final page. Press the "Menu" button, select "Go to" and select the "End" button.
You can rate a book even if you haven't linked your Amazon.com account to your social media accounts. Ratings are displayed at https://kindle.amazon.com/your_reading.
Note: You can only rate Kindle books purchased from the Kindle Store.

Book Recommendations

When you're finished reading a Kindle book, you'll see recommendations for similar books on the last page of the book. Recommendations are based on what other customers who bought this book also purchased.

To see these recommendations at any time, press Menu while reading. Select "Go to" and choose "End." Select a recommendation from this page to go directly to the recommended book's detail page in the Kindle Store.

Browsing The Web

Your Kindle comes with an experimental application called Web Browser. It supports JavaScript, SSL and cookies, but does not support media plug-ins (Flash, Shockwave, etc.) or Java applets. Most Amazon.com web pages can be viewed on your Kindle.

To launch Web Browser: Select "Launch Browser" from the Experimental screen or follow a link from within your reading material.

To launch Web Browser via search: Press the Menu button, select Search. Begin typing in the search box and use the 5-way controller to search by "Google," "Wikipedia" or "go to web."

Using the Basic Web Menu
To view the menu, press the Menu button when the Web Browser is open. Here's a list of options you'll find:

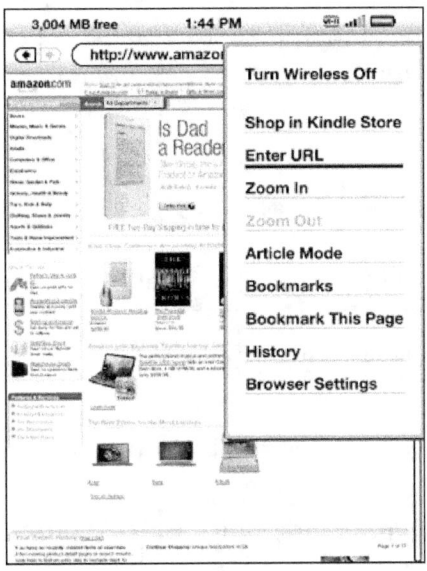

- Turn Wireless Off: Turns the Wireless connection off. If you turn the wireless off, you will not be able to use the browser.
- Shop in Kindle Store: Takes you to the Kindle Store.
- Enter URL: Takes you directly to the URL field where you can enter a web address to visit.
- Go to Top: Returns you to the top of the current web page.
- Bookmarks: Displays your list of web bookmarks.
- Bookmark This Page: Adds the current page to the bottom of your list of bookmarks.
- History: Displays your History page, which keeps track of the sites you have visited.
- Browser Settings: Displays options for clearing history and cookies, and disabling Javascript and images.
- Zoom: Zoom in and out of web pages.

Entering a URL

The URL text field retains the last URL you entered in case you want to quickly edit the same address and submit it again. If you want to enter a secure site with an "https" address, use the backspace key to delete the automatically entered "://" and type the address you want.

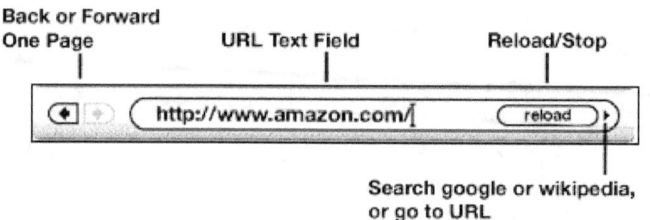

To enter the URL for a website:

    1.   Type in your URL when the cursor is visible in the URL text field.

    2.   When you are done typing, press the "Enter" button to view that website.

The URL text field is embedded in a navigation bar with a few other key shortcuts. To the right of the URL text field there is a button to stop loading or reload the current page. From there, move your 5-way controller to the right, and you can quickly search Google for the text entered in the URL text field.

Using Bookmarks and Adding Your Own

Bookmarks let you easily access a website without needing to type the address every time. When you open Web Browser from the experimental page for the first time, you will see a list of default bookmarks with links to information such as daily news. While browsing, you can also access the same list of bookmarks by selecting "Bookmarks" from the browser menu (just press the Menu button).

To add a website to the Bookmarks page:

    1.   Navigate to the site that you want to bookmark.

    2.   Press the Menu button and select "Bookmark This

Page."

To remove a bookmark:

    1.   Press the Menu button and select "Bookmarks."

    2.   Highlight the bookmark with the 5-way controller.

    3.   Move the 5-way controller to the left and select "delete bookmark."

To edit a bookmark: You can change the name of a bookmark by moving the 5-way controller to the right and selecting "edit bookmark." This only allows you to change the name of the bookmark. If you want to edit the URL, delete the bookmark and add a new one.

Using Next Page and Previous Page

Most web pages have more content than can be displayed on one page. Use the Next Page and Previous Page buttons to move through these pages. This is equivalent to using your mouse on a computer to move up and down through a web page. You can also move the cursor down with the 5-way controller until it reaches the bottom of the page.

Zooming in on a Web Page

While viewing a web page, press the Menu button and choose Zoom In or Zoom Out. If you see a magnifying glass displayed on a web page, you can use it to magnify a specific area of that web page.

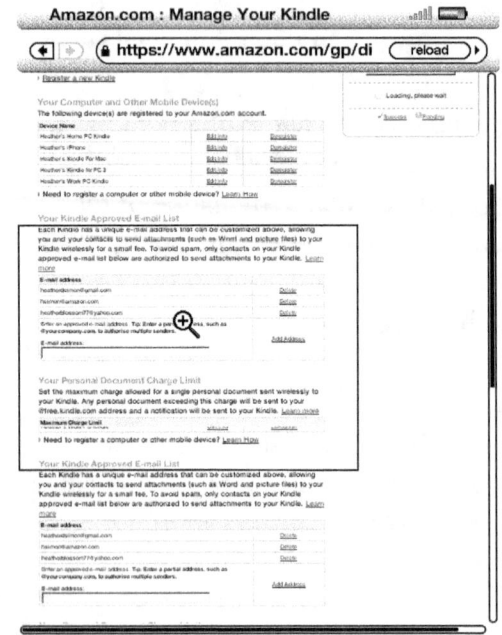

You can also choose where to zoom in using the 5-way controller:

1.   Use the 5-way controller to position the magnifying glass over the area that you want to magnify. (The magnifying glass is only available in portrait screen rotation.)

2.   Press the 5-way to zoom into the web page.

Note: To see more zoom options, press the Text key.

Selecting Links, Buttons, and Boxes

Navigate to links on a web page using the 5-way controller. Highlight the link you want to go to and press the 5-way controller to open the page.

Use the 5-way controller like you would use your mouse to navigate the web page. To enter information in an input field in a web page, move the cursor to that input field and begin typing.

Using History

You can easily return to websites you recently viewed by pressing the Menu button and selecting "History." You will then see a list of recently visited websites to select from. As noted above, you can also use this list to add a site to your Bookmarks by moving the 5-way to the right.

Downloading Files

Some websites may have books or documents you can download and read on your Kindle. When you select these books or documents using Web Browser, you will be asked to confirm if you want to download these to your Kindle Home screen. The types of files you can download include Kindle content (.AZW, .AZW1), unprotected Mobipocket books (.MOBI, .PRC), and text files (.TXT).

Web Browser Settings

You can modify the default browser behaviours and perform

simple maintenance procedures using Basic Web Settings. To display the Settings screen, press the Menu button while in the browser and then use the 5-way to select "Settings."

•   Clear Cache: Removes temporary Internet files from your Kindle. Move the on-screen highlight to "Clear Cache" and move the 5-way controller to the right.

•   Clear History: Removes cached Internet address entries from your Kindle. Move the on-screen highlight to "Clear History" and press the 5-way controller to clear this list.

•   Clear Cookies: Removes cookies from your Kindle. Move the on-screen highlight to "Clear Cookies" and press the 5-way to remove the cookies.

•   Enable Javascript: Enables or disables Javascript to be executed on the pages you visit. Note that if Javascript is disabled, Web pages will load faster.

- Disable Images: Select whether you want images to appear when you load a Web page. Note that if you do not show images, web pages will load faster.

Kindle Store

Shopping the Kindle Store on your Kindle is a convenient way to find and buy Kindle books, newspapers, magazines, and if you are a U.S. customer, Kindle active content and blogs for your Kindle. If you are in the Whispernet coverage area, your purchases from the Kindle Store are delivered to your Kindle, typically in less than 60 seconds. Books you purchase are automatically stored in your Kindle library on Amazon.com. Books available for re-download appear in your Archived Items when you remove them from your Kindle. Additional information is available on the Your Kindle Library Content Help page.

How to connect to the kindle Store

If you are in an area where wireless coverage is available, you have direct access to the Kindle Store on your Kindle through the built-in wireless feature. This allows you to purchase and download Kindle books, newspapers, magazines, and if you are a U.S. customer, blogs and Kindle active content right from your Kindle.

Note: If you are a U.S. customer using Kindle outside the U.S., please see Traveling with Your Kindle for more information.
To connect to the Kindle Store:

     1.   If wireless is not already on, press the Menu button and select "Turn Wireless On" using the 5-way controller.

     2.   Verify your connection by checking the connection status indicator in the upper right-hand corner of the Kindle screen.

     3.   Press the Menu button and select "Shop in Kindle Store" using the 5-way controller.

Navigating the Kindle Store

The Kindle Store and menu both provide multiple options for discovering books and periodicals. The storefront, titles, and prices you see may vary depending on your country or region. See Viewing and Updating Your Country or Region and Using Kindle if You Live Outside the United States for more information. Blogs and Kindle active content are not available outside the United States.

Searching the Kindle Store

The quickest path to finding what you want in the store is to search for keywords such as the author or title. The Search box is always visible at the bottom of every page in the Kindle Store.

To search the Kindle Store:

    1.   Type your search term. It will automatically appear in Search box regardless of where the cursor is positioned on the page.

    2.   Select "search store" using the 5-way controller.

Trying a Sample Book

Most Kindle books allow you to download a sample before you decide to buy the item.

To download a sample: Select "Try a Sample" from any product detail page that offers this option.

The end of the sample book has a link to revisit the product detail page for the item or a link to purchase the item directly. In addition, while reading a sample, the menu shows "Buy this Book Now" so you can purchase the sample at any time during your reading.

Setting Your Kindle Payment Method

When you buy books or other items directly from your Kindle, you're paying with the Default 1-click Payment Method on your Amazon.com account. Typically, this is the payment method associated with your default shipping address. For digital purchases, you can use a credit or debit card or Amazon Gift Cards.

To check or change your payment method:

1.   Go to Kindle Payment Settings on the Manage Your Kindle page.

2.   Click on "Edit" to update your payment method, then follow the on-screen instructions for choosing or adding a payment method.

3.   Click the "Continue" button to verify your changes.
Updating 1-Click Settings for Gift Card Purchases
You are not required to have a credit or debit card on your Amazon.com account to make digital purchases such as Kindle books, but you must establish a default 1-Click billing address on your Amazon.com account to use Amazon.com gift cards for digital purchases. If you don't already have a 1-Click billing address on your account, follow the instructions below to add an address without entering a credit or debit card to your account.
To add a 1-Click Billing Address for Gift Card purchases:

1.   Visit the <u>Manage Addresses and 1-Click Settings</u> page in Your Account.

2.   Click the Enter a new address button.

3.   Enter the address information and click the Continue button.

Set the address as your default by clicking the link on the address labeled "Click here to make this your 1-Click default address." You may be prompted to associate a credit or debit card with the address, but entering one of these payment methods is not required.

Redeeming Amazon.com Gift Cards

You must first redeem a Gift Card to Your Account. The funds the will be applied automatically to your next Kindle book purchase on your Kindle or from the Kindle Store on Amazon.com. Your Gift Card balance cannot be used to pay for books sold from the publisher or content with recurring subscription charges.

To redeem a Gift Card to Your Account:

1.   Visit the <u>Your Account</u> page.

2.   Click "Apply a Gift Card to your account."

3.   Sign in with your e-mail address and password.

4.   Enter your claim code and click "Redeem now." Your funds will automatically be applied to your next order.

Shopping for Kindle Content

After you've set up the payment method for your purchases from the Kindle Store (see <u>Setting Your Kindle Payment Method</u>), you're ready to shop for content. If your Kindle is connected wirelessly you can start shopping from your Kindle right away. You can also visit the Kindle Store on Amazon.com and send your purchases wirelessly (using 3G or Wi-Fi) to your Kindle, or download to your computer and transfer content using the USB connection. These Help pages will get you started:

- <u>Shopping for Kindle Content</u>

- <u>Transferring, Downloading, and Sending Files to Kindle</u>

Setting a Password on Kindle

If you want to make sure that only authorised users will have access to your Kindle, you can set a password on the Settings screen. You'll then need to enter the password to access your Kindle if it enters sleep mode or is turned off.

Tip: If your Kindle password contains characters or numbers not present on the Kindle keyboard, press the Symbol key to see a menu of additional characters.

To set your Kindle password:

1. Navigate to your Kindle's Home screen and press the Menu button.
2. Select "Settings" from the Home screen menu.
3. Select the "turn on" option next to Device Password on the Settings page.
4. Enter your new password twice and also enter a hint to help you remember the password.
5. Select "Submit" when you're finished.

If you wish to change or turn off your password in the future, navigate to the Settings menu again and select the available options.

Note: If you forget your password, move the 5-way controller down to view your password hint. Your Kindle will also give you the Kindle Support phone number so we can help reset your Kindle password.

Subscriptions ! What and how to manage it ?

Items Available Via Subscription

•   Periodicals: Periodicals include newspapers and magazines. Each periodical will be listed by its title on the Home screen and you can select that title to see all issues of the periodical you have on your Kindle.

•   Blogs: Blogs appear on the Home screen as a single entry like books. When you check for new items, your Kindle will download the complete feed so you can read your blogs offline.

Enriched Newspaper Editions

The enriched edition of Kindle newspapers includes all images provided by the publisher and can be downloaded via Wi-Fi to your Kindle.

You can still access your Kindle subscription content via a 3G connection, but this version may have a restricted number of images. The enriched edition is not available on Kindle 1st Generation and Kindle 2nd Generation devices.

Kindle newspapers delivered to Kindle applications always include all images provided by the publisher. Kindle subscription content is currently available for Kindle for Android and Kindle for iPhone/iPad/iPod touch.

Navigating Within a Periodical

At the bottom of a newspaper or magazine you will see options for quickly navigating within an issue. When viewing a blog, you will see similar options for navigation.

Clip This Article -- makes a copy of the entire article and adds it to your "My Clippings" file.

Keep This Issue -- designates the newspaper or magazine issue as one to be stored in your Kindle until you remove it. Once selected, this option changes to Do Not Keep This Issue.

Prev article -- takes you to the previous article.

View Sections & Articles -- takes you to the section list of a newspaper or magazine when you press the 5-way.

View Articles List -- takes you to the article list of a newspaper, magazine or blog when you press the 5-way.

Next article -- advances you to the next article.

◄ prev article　　**View Sections & Articles**　　next article ▶

By default, "View Sections & Articles for newspapers and magazines is highlighted and when you press the 5-way, a list of the sections with article summaries will appear. If you are viewing a blog, "View Articles List" is highlighted and pressing the 5-way shows a list of the blog's articles.

* * *

The New York Times

Sections 1 - 11 of 11		Articles 1 - 5 of 15
Front Page	(5)	Memo From Paris:
• International	(15)	France's Pain Over Algeria Reawakens With
National	(15)	2 New Films
Editorials, Op-Ed and Letters	(12)	Egypt Tries to Calm Ire Over Attack at Coptic
Business Day	(18)	Mass
Sports Tuesday	(21)	African Leaders Fail to Resolve Ivory Coast
The Arts	(16)	Standoff
Science Times	(24)	2 U.S. Service Members
Most E-Mailed	(14)	Are Killed in Iraq
New York	(11)	Judges Set to Rule on Afghan Election
Obituaries	(2)	Complaints Within 2 Weeks

prev | next

View Articles List

In the Sections & Articles view, you see the headlines of all the articles in each section. To see the Articles List of a particular section, navigate using the 5-way to "View Articles List" at the bottom of the screen.

* * *

To navigate to a particular article within a section or blog, simply move the 5-way controller to underline the article title and press to select.

Keeping Subscription Content

Older issues of newspapers and magazines appear inside a grouping called "Periodicals: Back Issues." Selecting the grouping takes you to a screen that displays the back issues you have on your Kindle.

Kindle automatically deletes issues that are more than seven issues old to free up space for new content. An exclamation point next to an issue indicates that it will be deleted soon. If you'd like to keep a copy of an issue, follow these steps:

To keep a back issue:

1. Open the specific issue from the Kindle Home screen.

2. Press the Menu button and select "Keep This Issue."

You will then see the word "keep" to the left of the issue title in

Home.

Keeping Subscription Content

Older issues of newspapers and magazines appear inside a grouping called "Periodicals: Back Issues." Selecting the grouping takes you to a screen that displays the back issues you have on your Kindle.

Kindle automatically deletes newspaper and magazine issues that are more than seven issues old to free up space for new content. An exclamation point next to a magazine or newspaper issue indicates that it will be deleted soon. If you'd like to keep a copy of an issue, follow these steps:

To keep a back issue:

1. Open the specific issue from the Kindle Home screen.
2. Press the Menu button and select "Keep This Issue."

You will then see the word "keep" to the left of the issue title in Home.

Travelling with your kindle

Battery Life

With Kindle's long battery life, you can read your Kindle device for up to 10 days with wireless on. Turn wireless off and read for up to one month. Battery life will vary based on wireless usage, such as shopping the Kindle Store and downloading content.

Charging Kindle's Battery Outside USA

Kindle always ships with a Kindle micro-USB cable that allows you to charge Kindle from a computer. To some countries, Kindle also ships with a U.S. power adapter. Power adapters for other countries are also available and can be added to your Kindle order at the time of purchase or bought separately. Please visit the Kindle Store to see the available options:

- Europe: http://www.amazon.com/gp/product/B002Y27P5K
- United Kingdom: http://www.amazon.com/gp/product/B002Y27P6E
- Australia: http://www.amazon.com/gp/product/B002Y27P50

You can charge your Kindle by connecting it to your computer via the Kindle micro-USB cable or by connecting it to a wall socket using the Kindle micro-USB cable and the Kindle power adapter plug appropriate for your country. The light on your Kindle next to the USB socket will appear yellow when charging and change to green when Kindle is fully charged.

Note on third-party charging devices (not included with your Kindle): Third-party charging devices, power converters, USB wall chargers, and other charging hubs are not supported nor recommended for your Kindle.

Charging from Your Computer via Kindle Micro-USB Cable

When using the Kindle micro-USB cable to charge your Kindle via your computer, charging time will normally take four to six hours. To charge your Kindle from a computer via Kindle micro-USB cable:

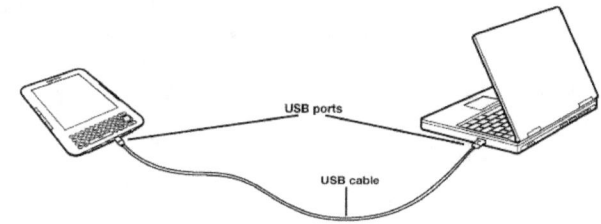

•

•   Connect Kindle directly to a USB port on your computer. Do not connect through a hub, keyboard, or monitor.

•   Connect Kindle to a computer plugged into a power outlet. We recommend keeping your computer plugged into a power outlet while charging your Kindle. Your computer may not supply sufficient power to the USB port if it is not plugged in.

•   Make sure your computer stays on during the entire charging process. Disable Standby, Hibernate or Sleep mode, if necessary.

•   Verify Kindle recognises the USB connection. You can verify your Kindle is charging if you see the USB drive mode screen. If you do not see this screen, unplug and reconnect your Kindle. You may also need to select an alternate USB port.

* * *

Using Kindle while Charging via Kindle Micro-USB Cable
You can use your Kindle while it is connected via USB and charging from your computer by unmounting or ejecting it so Kindle exits USB drive mode.

• Windows Vista and 7: Click on the Start button, select "Computer" from the options, right-click on the Kindle drive icon and select "Eject" from the pop-up menu.

• Windows XP: Right-click on the "Safely remove hardware" icon in the lower left-hand corner of the task bar and follow the on-screen instructions to remove Kindle.

• Mac OS: Cmd-click on the Kindle device icon and choose "Eject."

Kindle will then exit USB drive mode and display the Home screen. You'll see a lightning bolt on the battery status icon that indicates your Kindle is still charging.

Shopping and Downloading on Amazon.com!

If you're traveling outside the wireless service area or prefer to use your Kindle without accessing wireless services, you can still shop in the Kindle Store on Amazon.com. See Shopping the Kindle Store on Amazon.com for more information.

To download items to your computer at the time of purchase:

1.	Select "Transfer via Computer" from the Deliver to: pull-down menu on the product detail page.

2.	Save the file to your computer when prompted by your web browser.

3.	Connect Kindle to your computer with the USB cable.

4.	Use your computer's file browser to drag and drop the file to your Kindle.

Downloading Archived Content without Wireless

Books you purchase are automatically stored in your Kindle Library on Amazon.com. Books available for re-download appear on the Manage Your Kindle page. Additional information is available on the Your Kindle Library Content Help page.

To download your items from Manage Your Kindle:

1. Visit the <u>Manage Your Kindle</u> page.
2. Locate the item you wish to download in the "Your Orders " section at the bottom of the page. If you have a lot of content, you may need to use the Previous and Next options at the bottom to navigate through all of your content.
3. Click on "Deliver to. . ." next to the title and choose "Transfer via Computer" from the list.
4. Save the file to your computer when prompted by your web browser.
5. Connect Kindle to your computer with the USB cable.
6. Use your computer's file browser to drag and drop the file to your Kindle.

For more information on using your Kindle's USB connection and transferring files from your computer to your Kindle, see the <u>Transferring, Downloading, and Sending Files to Kindle</u> Help page.

Transferring Personal Documents without Wireless Service

To access your personal documents for free on your Kindle, send attachments to "name"@free.kindle.com. We'll send the files to your Kindle via Wi-Fi and and also e-mail them to the address associated with your Amazon.com account. Alternatively, you can transfer the documents to your Kindle using your USB connection. To learn more, see Transferring, Downloading, and Sending Files to Kindle.

Wireless Coverage Map

Visit the <u>Kindle product page</u> to view the coverage map for your device and location.

Kindle Users Living Outside the United States

If you live outside the United States and use Kindle, please see <u>Using Kindle if You Live Outside the United States</u>.

International Service Fees

Kindle customers from the United States can travel internationally and still get books in less than 60 seconds. Customers have the option to wirelessly receive periodicals and personal documents for a fee, or transfer files from their computer for free.

• International Subscription Service: Receive all of your newspaper, magazine, and blog subscription content wirelessly for a weekly fee of $4.99.

• International Personal Document Service: Transfer personal documents to your Kindle wirelessly for $.99 per megabyte (rounded up to the next whole megabyte). For more information about transferring personal files to your Kindle, see the Transferring, Downloading, and Sending Files to Kindle Help page.

Transferring, Downloading, Sending Files to Kindle

Trensferring New Content to Kindle

If you already own a Kindle and Kindle content, you can download content to your new Kindle. Download your books and personal documents, directly from your new Kindle wirelessly and transfer subscriptions from the Manage Your Kindle page. Transfer personal documents, and MP3 and Audible files from your computer to your new Kindle Keyboard via USB.

Downloading Arechived Contents !

Kindle displays the items you've downloaded on the Home screen. If you have Kindle content or personal documents stored in your Kindle Library that aren't displayed, you can download them from Archived Items when your Kindle's wireless connection is turned on. Your purchases are also available for download on the Manage Your Kindle page. Additional information is available on the Your Kindle Library Content Help page.

To download archived items:

     1.   Select "Archived Items" from the Home screen or "View Archived Items" from the menu.

     2.   Select the item from the Archived Items screen.

Transferring Periodical Subscriptions

To transfer a periodical subscription for delivery of future issues from one Kindle to another, follow these steps:

1.   From your computer's web browser, go to the <u>Manage Your Kindle</u> page.

2.   Scroll down to the section entitled Your Active Kindle subscriptions.

3.   Under "Deliver future editions," select the Kindle to which you'd like the subscription to be transferred, and then select "Save."

4.   Upon publication of the next issue, the periodical will appear in the designated Kindle.

Downloading Archived contents without Wireless !

If you are traveling outside your Free 3G service area, you can still download your Kindle content purchased from Amazon.com to your computer and transfer it via USB or Wi-Fi to your Kindle. To download items archived on Amazon.com to your computer with Wi-Fi, press the Menu button and select Turn Wireless On. If a Wi-Fi network has been set up and is within range, your Kindle will use the Wi-Fi connection by default. If you need assistance configuring your Wi-Fi network, visit the Wireless on Your Kindle Help page.

To download items archived on Amazon.com to your computer:

1. Visit the Manage Your Kindle page.
2. Scroll to the Your orders section and locate the item you wish to download.
3. Click on the Deliver to pull-down menu and select Transfer via Computer.
4. Select the Kindle your wish to transfer the file to and click the "Download to computer" button.
5. Choose Save file when prompted by your Web browser.
6. Follow the instructions in the "Transferring Files Via USB" section below to place the file onto your Kindle.
7. Click Close on the Manage Your Kindle page when the file is done downloading.

Kindle ME

Transferring Files via USB

Both Macintosh and Windows users can download and transfer
Kindle content, personal documents, and MP3 and Audible files
from their computers to their Kindle through the USB cable. When
your Kindle is plugged into your computer, your Kindle will
appear as a removable mass-storage device.

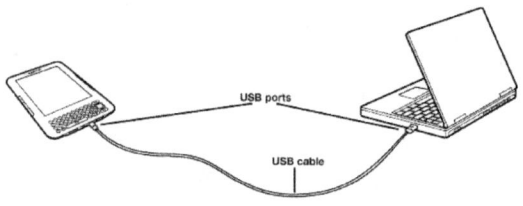

Sending Personal Documents to Kindle

Kindle Personal Documents service makes it easy to take your personal documents with you, eliminating the need to print. Kindle Personal Document Service allows you to:

- Read your personal documents on your Kindle Keyboard. You and your approved contacts can send personal documents to your Kindle Keyboard using your Send-to-Kindle e-mail address.

- Store your personal documents in your Kindle Library. You can download your archived personal documents to your Kindle device conveniently anywhere, at any time. These documents will be stored in your Kindle Library until you delete them from Manage Your Kindle.

- Create bookmarks and annotations on your personal documents. Just as with Kindle books, Whispersync automatically synchronises your last page read, bookmarks, and annotations for personal documents (with the exception of PDFs) across your Kindles.

Detailed information on Kindle Personal Document service is available on our Kindle Personal Document Service help page. You and your approved contacts can e-mail personal documents to your Kindle Keyboard through your Send-to-Kindle e-mail address. You must ensure that:

- You have approved the sender's e-mail address Learn

More
- You gave the sender your Send-to-Kindle e-mail address. Learn More
- Your document is a supported file type. Learn More
The documents will be sent to your Kindle Keyboard and also be stored in your Kindle library if your Personal Document Archive settings have been enabled. Learn More.
For detailed instructions on topics such as Sending Personal Documents to Kindle, Setting up Approved Contacts, Supported File Types view our Kindle Personal Document Services help page.
Finding the Send-to-Kindle e-mail address on your Kindle Keyboard
The Send-to-Kindle e-mail address associated with your Kindle Keyboard will be displayed on the Kindle Keyboard's Settings screen.
1. Press the Menu button and select Settings.
2. Your Kindle's [name]@kindle.com e-mail address is listed under the Send-to-Kindle E-mail heading.

* * *

Personal Document Delivery Fees for Kindle Keyboard 3G
Fees for transfer of personal documents to Kindle Keyboard via Whispernet are based on the size of the file submitted (before compression if you use a .zip file), your country, and where you're accessing Whispernet. Fees will only be charged for documents that are successfully received wirelessly to your Kindle Keyboard. (Personal Document Service is not available via Whispernet in Canada. Please see Sending Personal Documents to Kindle for information about e-mailing personal documents to your computer for USB transfer to your Kindle.)

- Kindle (U.S. Wireless) user: We'll send personal documents to your Kindle Keyboard via Whispernet while inside the U.S. wireless coverage area for a fee of $.15 per megabyte.

- Kindle (Free 3G) user living in the United States: If you transfer personal documents to your Kindle Keyboard via Whispernet while inside the United States, the fee is $ .15 per megabyte. When traveling outside the United States, a fee of $.99 per megabyte will apply.

- Kindle (Free 3G) user living outside the United States: We'll send personal files to your Kindle Keyboard via Whispernet for a fee of $ .99 (USD) per megabyte anywhere in the world you access Whispernet service.

Fees are rounded up to the next whole MB and apply to each personal document delivered via Whispernet to each Kindle. You can transfer personal documents to your Kindle via USB for free at anytime.

Aggregation of Fees for Personal Document Service
Consecutive orders for Personal Document Service via Whispernet that cost less than $5.00 may be combined into one transaction and appear as a single charge on your credit or debit card billing statement.

Setting your Personal Document Charge Limit
Sending Personal Documents to Kindle

* * *

On the <u>Manage Your Kindle</u> page you can set the maximum charge allowed for a single personal document sent wirelessly to your Kindle Keyboard. Any personal document exceeding this charge will be stored in your Kindle Library if your personal document archive settings have been enabled and will be available for download at a later date from your Archived Items on your Kindle Keyboard.

To set the Charge Limit for Personal Document Service:

- Visit the <u>Manage Your Kindle</u> page.
- Select Personal Document Settings from the left hand menu.
- Scroll down to the heading "Whispernet Delivery Options."
- Select "Edit" on the right hand side of the page.
- Enter your preferred personal document charge limit.
- Click "Update."

The limit you set is a per document limit. If you send multiple documents for conversion in a .ZIP file, the total aggregated charge for conversion of all the documents may exceed your per document limit. As long as each document's charge is below the limit, conversion and delivery will be successful.

To change the Delivery Options for Personal Document Service:

- Visit the <u>Manage Your Kindle</u> page.
- Select Personal Document Settings from the left hand menu.
- Scroll down to the heading "Whispernet Delivery Options".
- Select "Edit" on the right hand side of the page.
- Un-tick the box stating "Enable delivery to my Kindle over Whispernet. Fees apply".
- Click "Update".

For detailed screen shots please see our <u>Manage Your Kindle on</u>

Amazon.com help page.

Downloadiing to Multiple Devices

Content purchased from the Kindle Store can be downloaded to your Kindle Keyboard, or Kindle compatible device, as long as you've registered the device to the Amazon.com account that purchased the Kindle content. There is no limit on the number of times a title can be downloaded to a registered device, but there may be limits on the number of devices (usually 6) that can simultaneously use a single book.

That means you can download and read your books on any Kindle device you own as long you've registered each device to the Amazon.com account where your Kindle Library is stored.

You can see the items in your Kindle Library under Archived Items on your Kindle and send downloads to your registered Kindles from the "Your Orders" section of the Manage Your Kindle page.

What Files Kindle Recognizes ?!

You can purchase and wirelessly download Kindle books, newspapers, magazines and blogs from the Kindle Store as well as download and read other types of non-DRM (Digital Rights Management) text-based content on your Kindle. You can also play Audible audiobooks or MP3 files. When your Kindle Keyboard is connected to a computer and mounted as a USB drive, you will see three default directories or folders. Here's a list of the directories and the file types recognised by Kindle Keyboard:

- Documents: Kindle (.AZW, .AZW1). Text (.TXT), Unprotected Mobipocket (.MOBI, .PRC)
- Audible: Audible (.AA, .AAX)
- Music: MP3 (.MP3)

Mobipocket files must have no Digital Rights Management (DRM) protection applied to be readable on your Kindle Keyboard. If you purchased a Mobipocket file from a Mobipocket retailer, you will not be able to open the file on your Kindle. EPUB eBooks are not supported on Kindle.

You can add any of the above file types to your Kindle without using the Personal Document Service to convert those files to a compatible type. If it is not listed above, conversion would be necessary to read the file on the Kindle Keyboard.

Built-in PDF Reader for Kindle Keyboard, Kindle (2nd Generation), and Kindle DX devices

Your Kindle displays most PDF documents without losing the formatting of the original file. You can magnify PDFs by viewing them in landscape mode.

To zoom on a PDF document:

1. Press the Text key.
2. Select the zoom percentage from the available options.
3. Position the zoom box over the section you'd like to view using the 5-way controller and press to select.

You'll see scroll bars appear at the edges of the page that indicate what section you're viewing. Use the 5-way controller to move across the page and view different sections. To return to the previous view, press the Text key and select fit-to-screen.

Troubleshooting Your Kindle

Registration Issues

Symptom	Resolution
I don't know how to register my Kindle.	You can register your Kindle online or straight from the device itself. To register your Kindle online:

You can register your Kindle online or straight from the device itself.
To register your Kindle online:

1.   Go to the Manage Your Kindle page.

2.   Enter the 16-digit serial number of your Kindle (Tip: It starts with "B00").

3.   Click on "Register a new Kindle."

To register your Kindle on the device:

1.   Press the Home button; then press the Menu button and select Turn Wireless On.

2.   Press Menu again and navigate to "Settings" using the 5-way controller; press to select.

3.   If you received Kindle as a gift, and the person who gave it to you is listed as the "Registered User," select "deregister."

4.   Select "register."

•   If you have an Amazon account: Enter the e-mail address and password of your Amazon.com account. Navigate to "submit" using the 5-way controller; then press to select. Your name will appear as the "Registered User" when registration

Michael Haridy

Screen Issues

Symptom	Resolution
Kindle screen frozen or Kindle unresponsive. *Possible cause:* • Low battery charge.	1. Reset your Kindle by sliding and holding the power switch for 20 seconds. Release the power switch. The reboot screen will appear. 2. If Kindle is still unresponsive, try charging Kindle before resetting the device once again. 3. Make sure you have the latest software version available installed on your Kindle. The latest version is available here: www.amazon.com/ kindlesoftwareupdates If you continue to experience problems, please contact us.
Kindle showing lines on screen. *Possible cause:* • The Kindle may be affected by electromagnetic interference or screen may be defective.	Move and hold the power switch for 20 seconds before releasing it.

Michael Haridy

Broken Screen or Case

Symptom	Resolution
Kindle screen or case is cracked or broken.	See Kindle Return Policies to learn more about the warranty on your Kindle.

Wireless Issues

Symptom	Resolution
Wi-Fi Connection Issues Kindle is unable to connect to Wi-Fi network, or book, subscription, or blog will not download via Wi-Fi to Kindle.	Learn how to connect to Wi-Fi in four easy steps, and troubleshoot common problems.
Free 3G Connection Issues Kindle is unable to connect to 3G, or book, subscription, or blog will not download via 3G to Kindle.	

Lost or Stolen Kindle

Symptom	Resolution
Lost or stolen Kindle.	First, deregister Kindle via the Manage Your Kindle page. If your Kindle is found and we're contacted, we'll arrange for it to be returned to you. To file a police report, please contact your local police department. You will also want to make sure that you cancel any active Kindle subscriptions on the Manage Your Kindle Subscriptions page. Cancelling the subscription will ensure that you are no longer billed; you'll also receive a pro-rated refund for remaining issues you already paid for. You always have the option of subscribing at a later date.
I found a Kindle.	Please contact us for instructions on how to send us the Kindle you found. We will contact the owner and return the Kindle to them.

Connecting Via USB

Symptom	Resolution
Kindle is not recognised by your computer or you receive an error message when you plug your Kindle into your computer. *Possible cause:* • Kindle not connected to a powered USB port.	First, disconnect Kindle from computer and try plugging it back in using a different USB port. You can also try using a different micro USB cable, if available. If it is still not working, follow these next steps: 1. Restart Kindle by pressing Home > Menu > Settings > Menu and select **Restart**. 2. Connect the Kindle to a USB port on the back of your computer. 3. Restart your computer with the Kindle connected to it. If these steps do not resolve the issue, you can reset your Kindle. Unplug your Kindle from the outlet or computer, slide and hold power button for 20 seconds, and wait for 5-10 minutes. Please contact us if you continue to experience problems with your Kindle.

Michael Haridy

Password Issues

Symptom	Resolution
Kindle password not working or lost.	Remember to use the shift button for uppercase letters, and use the Symbol key to insert numbers and other characters. If you cannot remember the password for your Kindle, you can reset your password to regain access. Resetting your password will delete all content on your Kindle and you'll need to register your Kindle again from the Settings screen before downloading items from your Kindle Library on Amazon.com. To reset your Kindle if you don't have the password: 1. Slide and release the power switch on the top of Kindle to turn on the device or exit sleep mode. 2. Enter "resetmykindle" in the password field and press the enter key on the key pad. 3. Wait several minutes while your Kindle restarts.

Kindle Account

Symptom	Resolution
Kindle does not have owner's name on home screen. *Possible cause:* • Kindle not registered, or registered to different account.	1. Deregister the Kindle. 2. Register the Kindle. Steps to deregister and register device can be found here. Note: The name on the Kindle will default to the first name on your Amazon.com account. You can change the name on the Manage Your Kindle page.

Power Issues

Symptom	Resolution
Kindle battery not charging.	1. Connect Kindle to a different outlet and/or USB port. If available, also try using a different USB cable or power adapter 2. Verify the yellow charge light in the power switch at the base of the Kindle is on. When fully charged, the light will appear green. 3. Restart Kindle by pressing Home > Menu > Settings > Menu and select "Restart." Is the charge light on? 4. Is the charge light off? AC adapter needs to be replaced. 5. Contact us for in-warranty options.
Kindle battery not holding a charge. *Possible cause:* 1. Kindle receiving a weak wireless signal and is constantly trying to connect. 2. A large number of files were recently added to the Kindle and the	

Wireless Issues

* * *

Symptom	Resolution
Wi-Fi Connection Issues Kindle is unable to connect to Wi-Fi network, or book, subscription, or blog will not download via Wi-Fi to Kindle.	Learn how to connect to Wi-Fi in four easy steps, and troubleshoot common problems.
Free 3G Connection Issues Kindle is unable to connect to 3G, or book, subscription, or blog will not download via 3G to Kindle. *Possible cause:* • The Kindle is not able to sync with Amazon.com.	1. Check battery (if low, charge before completing following steps). 2. Check that wireless is enabled (press Menu then Turn Wireless On). 3. Check for wireless strength. 4. Sync and check for items. 5. Check wireless coverage map. 6. Try restarting Kindle by pressing Home > Menu > Settings > Menu and select "Restart." 7. Sync and check for items.

Not able to

Music and Audible Files

Symptom	Resolution
Music files not playing on Kindle. *Possible cause:* • Music files not found by the Kindle or files not in supported format.	1. Plug your Kindle into a computer via the USB cable. 2. Kindle will be recognized as an external drive. 3. Click to open the Kindle drive. 4. Open the music folder. 5. Make sure all the music files are inside the music folder. 6. Confirm file extension is MP3 (right-click on file to see properties).
Cannot play audiobook. *Possible cause:* • Audio book may not be compatible with Kindle or could not be found.	1. Connect your Kindle to computer using USB cable 2. Kindle will be recognized as an external hard drive 3. Click on Kindle drive and select audible folder 4. Make sure audio book files are inside the audible folder 5. Confirm file type is audible by doing a right-click on the file and select properties. 6. Contact Audible

UntitledKindle Lighted Covers

Symptom	Resolution
• No LED lights ever come on • Not all LED lights come on • LED light flickers	1. Shut down the Kindle. Slide and hold the power button for five seconds. The LED light will blink three times and the screen will go blank. 2. Connect the cover to the Kindle. Refer to www.amazon.com/kindlecover. 3. Turn the Kindle on by sliding and releasing the power button. 4. If the Kindle does not power on: charge your Kindle for one hour, and attempt these steps again Please contact us if you continue to experience problems with your Kindle cover.

Contents Issues

Symptom	Resolution
Book did not download / haven't received book, subscription, or blog. *Possible cause:* • Kindle not able to sync with Amazon servers.	Try these troubleshooting steps: • Restart Kindle Keyboard by pressing Home > Menu > Settings > Menu and select Restart. • See Wireless Issues troubleshooting steps. • Transfer files manually via USB.
Cannot delete book from Kindle Keyboard.	1. Go to the Home screen. 2. Underline the book you want to delete. 3. Move the 5-way controller to the left. 4. Select "Delete."
Book will not open / receiving an error message when opening a book. *Possible cause:* • Incomplete file download.	1. Delete the book. 2. Restart your Kindle Keyboard by pressing Home > Menu > Settings > Menu and select "Restart." 3. Download book again. If you continue to experience problems, please contact us.

Kindle with Special Offers Issues

Symptom	Resolution
My screensaver says that I need to connect to Wi-Fi.	If you have recently performed a 20-second reboot, Kindle with Special Offers will display a screensaver indicating that you need to connect to Wi-Fi. Learn more about connecting to Wi-Fi. After successfully connecting to Wi-Fi, it may take up to five minutes for your Kindle to begin displaying special offers again. If you are still having problems, reset your Kindle by sliding and holding the power switch for 20 seconds. Release the power switch. The reboot screen will appear.
I clicked on "E-mail me more details" on an offer, but haven't received an e-mail about it.	First, make sure you've checked the e-mail account to which your Kindle is registered. It's the same e-mail address you use to login to your Amazon.com account. Check your junk mail folder. If you've verified that you are checking the correct e-mail account and you don't see the e-mail, please contact us for help.
When I clicked an offer, it wouldn't work.	The offers on your Kindle with Special Offers are updated frequently. To view all current offers, go to the Home

Contact Kindle Support

Location	Telephone Number
Inside the United States	You can reach us by phone directly and toll-free by clicking the "Contact Us" button in the right-hand column of the Kindle Support pages. Leave your number, and we'll call you right back. Direct toll-free number: 1-866-321-8851.

Selected Countries and U.S. Territories: • Australia • Canada • France • Germany • Guam • Hong Kong • Japan • Puerto Rico • United Kingdom • Virgin Islands	You can reach us by phone directly and toll free by clicking the "Contact Us" button in the right-hand column of our Kindle Support pages. Leave your number, and we'll call you right back. Direct number: 1-206-266-0927.
All Other Countries	Direct number: 1-206-266-0927.

Book Three

Get me
Free eBOOKS

Amazon Free ebooks

The Amazon Kindle Store lets you choose from limited-time promotional offers and thousands of the most popular classics all available for free with wireless delivery in under 60 seconds via Whispernet.

1. Visit Limited-time Promotional Offers or Kindle Popular Classics.

2. Browse for a title just like a normal Kindle ebook.

Internet Archive

Over 2.5 million free titles

Internet Archive is a non-profit dedicated to offering permanent access to historical collections that exist in digital format. Provides over 2.5 million free ebooks to read, download, and enjoy.

1. Visit archive.org.

2. Search for a title or browse one of the sub-collections like American Libraries.

3. When viewing a title, click the link on the left labeled "Kindle (beta)" to download the file to your computer.

4. Attach your Kindle to your computer using your USB cable and drag the file to the "Documents" folder on your Kindle. You can also e-mail the file to your Kindle using Whispernet for wireless delivery (charges may apply).

5. Open the ebook from your Kindle's home screen and enjoy.

Project Gutenberg

Over 36,000 free titles

Project Gutenberg, one of the original sources of free ebooks, is dedicated to the creation and distribution of eBooks.

1. Visit gutenberg.org.

2. Search for a title or browse the book shelves by topic.

3. When viewing a title, scroll down to the 'Download this ebook for free' section and click the download link for 'Mobipocket' or 'Mobipocket with images' format.

4. Attach your Kindle to your computer using your USB cable and drag the file to the "Documents" folder on your Kindle. You can also e-mail the file to your Kindle using Whispernet for wireless delivery (charges may apply).

5. Open the ebook from your Kindle's home screen and enjoy.

ManyBooks.net

Over 26,000 free titles

ManyBooks.net provides free ebooks as a service to the Internet community at large.

1. Visit manybooks.net.

2. Search for a title or browse by genre.

3. When viewing a title, choose the "Kindle (.azw)" option on the right hand side and click the 'Download' button.

4. Attach your Kindle to your computer using your USB cable and drag the file to the "Documents" folder on your Kindle. You can also e-mail the file to your Kindle using Whispernet for wireless delivery (charges may apply).

5. Open the ebook from your Kindle's home screen and enjoy.

Michael Haridy

LibriVox

Over 20,000 titles plus

provides free audiobooks from the public domain. There are
several options for listening. The first step is to get the mp3 or ogg
files your own computer:LibriVox provides free audiobooks from
the public domain. There are several options for listening. The first
step is to get the mp3 or ogg files into your own computer:
http://librivox.org/

Open Library

Over 1,000,000 free titles

The World's classic literature at your fingertips. Over 1,000,000 free ebook titles available . One web page for every book ever published. It's a lofty but achievable goal.

To build Open Library, we need hundreds of millions of book records, a wiki interface, and lots of people who are willing to contribute their time and effort to building the site.

To date, we have gathered over 20 million records from a variety of large catalogs as well as single contributions, with more on the way.

http://openlibrary.org/

Munseys

Over 20,000 free titles

if you own a portable reading device, Munseys is one of the places to go. They have ebooks you can use on the most common reading devices , and ALL of them are FREE !
http://www.munseys.com/

Google eBook Store

Google ebookstore

Over 1,000,000 free titles

The free section is filled with thousands of free, scanned copies of books, available in Kindle-friendly PDF formats.

http://books.google.com/ebooks?
hl=en&as_coll=1040&uid=2278874564547928826&source=gbs_s
lider_bookshelves_1040_webstore_home

World Library

Over 100,000 free titles

The World Public Library Association is the world's largest eBook provider. Founded in 1996, the World Public Library Association is a global coordinated effort to preserve and disseminate classic works of literature, serials, bibliographies, dictionaries, encyclopaedias, and other reference works in a number of languages and countries around the world. Their mission is to serve the public, aid students and educators by providing both free public access and an enhanced membership section to the world's most complete collection of electronic texts, books, and documents on-line as well as offer a variety of services and resources that support and strengthen the instructional programs of education, elementary through post baccalaureate studies.

http://worldlibrary.net/default.aspx

Public Domain

BookYards

Over 800,000 free titles

Bookyards says they are the "library to the world" and with their selection, one would certainly believe it. They have over 16,000 books, 800,000 ebooks, and 384 videos. There are 32,000 ebook links as well. These are all in different categories and they've added ten new categories such as Literature, War, and Games. This is a relatively easy to navigate website, with plenty of free ebooks to download.

Read more at Suite101: How to Get Free Kindle Ebooks: Online Electronic Books Free for the Download | Suite101.com http:// tinasamuels.suite101.com/how-to-get-free-kindle-ebooks-a98945#ixzz1cEqYYyf

http://www.bookyards.com/categories.html?type=books

Michael Haridy

FreeKindleBooks

Over 100,000 free titles

Free Kindle Books offers these E-books (below) under the same identical terms as Project Gutenberg. We consider these to be "the same books" as Project Gutenberg, file-format-converted to run natively on Kindle and other MOBI and PRC compatible E-Book Readers. Please read the terms of use before downloading. Recently Project Gutenberg has started supporting MOBI file format directly on an "experimental" basis, although the existence of these files is not correctly reported if you search on the "PRC" file type. The Project Gutenberg file conversion process to MOBI is different than that used by this website, so sometimes the PG version may be better for your purposes, and sometimes the E-Books on this site. The Project Gutenberg site remains difficult to use directly from Kindle. This site remains a great place to browse for great books from Kindle,If no size is given for a file, you may download it directly to Kindle. If a size is given (X Megs) please download these Free Books first to your computer desktop and then from there to your Kindle -- it will probably not work otherwise! (The large files include illustrations.)
Navigate by Author to your choice of E-book in Kindle-compatible MOBI or PRC format:

http://www.freekindlebooks.org/

Michael Haridy

Fictionwise

Over 10,000 free titles

Fictionwise is the top independent eBook seller in the world with
tens of thousands of satisfied customers. We offer award-winning
eBooks by top authors!

Try some of our free samples below, and check out the thousands
of other titles we offer by top authors!

http://www.fictionwise.com/ebooks/freebooks.htm?cache

Free OnLine Novels

Free-Online-Novels

.com

Over 100,000 free titles

Looking for a free novel? You will find here an extensive collection of links to free online novels, organised by genre (Adventure, Mystery, Romance... etc.) and alphabetically by title within each genre.

http://www.free-online-novels.com/index.html

Forgotten Books

Over 10,000 free titles

Forgotten Books! From this web site you can read literally thousands of books online, download free ebooks in PDF format, and if you prefer to read from paper, we sell high-quality paperback books at wholesale prices.
We are an independent publisher, specialising in historical writings. This includes works such as: classical fiction, philosophy, science, religion, folklore, mythology and sacred texts, in addition to secret and esoteric subjects, such as: occult, freemasonry, alchemy, hermetic and ancient knowledge. We have fiction and non-fiction books in both print and as e-books for download.
Forgotten Books is a book publisher. All of the books on this web site are published by us. We reprint classical literature and old books that have long been out of print. Many of our books you may not find elsewhere.
Forgotten Books is proud partner of Amazon.com and Google Books.

http://www.forgottenbooks.org/

BookRix

BookRix
web your book

Over 90,000 free titles

is just such a book lovers website, a community platform where you can read, rate and rant away on books. BookRix is also a place where new authors can present their own works. In that respect BookRix acts like an online publishing house for free via the medium of the browser.

http://www.bookrix.com/library.html

Justfreebooks

Over 3,000,000 free titles

JustFreeBooks search the content of more than 700 web sites ,
including Gutenbreg.org , wikibooks.org , and Archive.org .
With JustFreeBooks you can find all sorts of free books , public
domain books , free audio books and all sorts of books and more .
Just type in their search box the book , author , or theme you want
to find .

http://www.justfreebooks.info/

The FREE Library

Over 18,000 free titles

Since 2003, The Free Library has offered free, full-text versions of classic literary works from hundreds of celebrated authors, whose biographies, images, and famous quotations can also be found on the site. Recently, The Free Library has been expanded to include a massive collection of periodicals from hundreds of leading publications covering Business and Industry, Communications, Entertainment, Health, Humanities, Law, Government, Politics, Recreation and Leisure, Science and Technology, and Social Sciences. This collection includes millions of articles dating back to 1984 as well as newly-published articles that are added to the site daily.

http://www.thefreelibrary.com/

vook ! Read it , Watch it !

Vook is the leading mixed-media digital producer that lights up the world's content and connects people around stories and ideas that they love. A vook is a new innovation in reading that blends a well-written book, high-quality video and the power of the Internet into a single, complete story. You can read your book, watch videos that enhance the story, and connect with authors and your friends through social media all on one screen, without switching between platforms.

Vook has recently partnered with authors such as Charles River Editors, Thomas J. Murrey, Alycea Ungaro, and Gemma Quinn to create Brief Histories, Textvooks, How-To Guides, and quick guides. Some of their bestselling products include:

-New York: A Brief History
-Astronomy: The Quick Guide
-Everyday Pilates: From the Top Down
-50 Soups (Cooking in America)
-Caring For Your Toddler (1-3 year old): The Video Quide

http://www.amazon.com/Vook/e/B005CAKPF8/
ref=ntt_dp_epwbk_0

Michael Haridy

Book Four

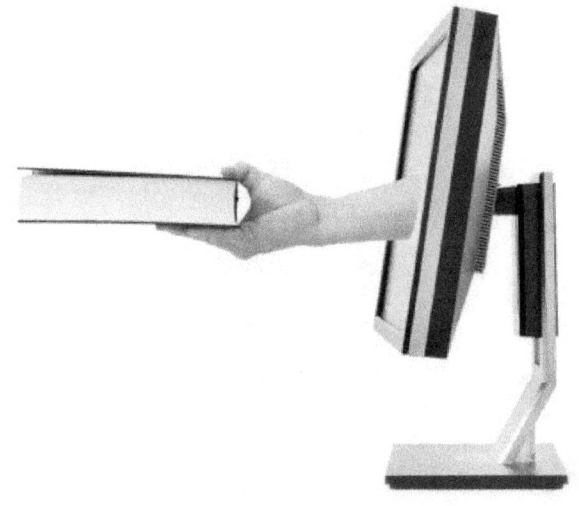

Things No One
will tell you about

Michael Haridy

Features in the Kindle 4 You Didn't Know About

10 Things You Need to Know !

If you have just heard about the entire latest buzz surrounding the e-book reader Kindle from Amazon, you need to know more. Here are the top 10 aspects about Kindle almost everyone needs to know!

MP3 playing

The Kindle device from Amazon has the amazing ability to play all the MP3 songs which you would have downloaded into the internal storage mechanism. Capacities of the internal storage are around 180 MB in space. You could also store these MP3 songs in the allocated SD card slot. You can play the songs in random shuffle and choose to listen to songs in the background while you read the e-book!

DRM support

The Kindle comes with DRM support by means of support for file types of extensions .AZW. It also is compatible with Mobipocket books of the unprotected varieties. Therefore file types like .MOBI, .TXT, .PRC, Word as well as .HTML are all supported by the Kindle. You can transfer files via USB or via email. No more need to print!

Search for free

This is a new feature introduced by Kindle which enables a powerful search mechanism. By means of a query mechanism you can search for almost anything you wish for absolutely free of cost! This search facility is powered with the help of Mechanical

Turn from Amazon which is a distributed system of work.

Blog subscription

You can avail blog subscriptions by paying a $2 dollars every month! Besides this, you also get access to a 14 day trial period. For no additional cost, you get to browse the blogs directly via the 'Basic Web' which is a browser provided for free. You only pay for access to the RSS feeds but not for surfing the web.

Font types supported

Kindle primarily supports two kinds of fonts namely the Neue Helvetica and the Caecilia. These are provided by Linotype. Book texts are all provided in the default Caecilia font. However, other than reading, you can select from 6 font types.

Ergonomics

While the Kindle may not have great aesthetics what with a no-so-great looking the shape of the device is very ergonomically designed.

No scroll keys

If you wish to navigate to the next page or further below, there are no scroll down keys provided in the Kindle. To move across content or even scrolling on the web pages you will need to use the page forward keys and the back button for this.

Audible e-books

You can use the Kindle from Amazon to play out audible e-books. However the 'whispernet' service provided by means of the EVDO internet connection does not support downloads of such audible e-books on air. You will need to leverage the Audible Manager for downloading and subsequently copy the file to Kindle via USB port on the PC. This eliminates the need for printing altogether.

* * *

Text file download
Kindle allows you to easily download text files for future use. All it takes is just 45 seconds to download even massive text files!

Files not supported
The Kindle does not ensure compatibility with Mobipocket files which have been DRMed. Also the Kindle will not support PDF file types – not even after you convert the file!

10 Features you don't know about !

The Kindle has a microphone
According to the manual, the microphone is currently disabled.
But what will it do in the future? Could we be dictating notes to
our Kindles someday? Just wait till the hackers dig into this one.

Free PDF document delivery
To email a PDF to your Kindle, but avoid any kind of 3G delivery
fees, tack @ free.kindle.com onto your email address. The file
will only be downloaded over Wi-Fi.

Wi-Fi Audible delivery
Audible audio books can be transferred to the Kindle over Wi-Fi,
no computer necessary. The Kindle will also automatically shut off
3G service when connected to Wi-Fi for faster downloads.

More PDF enhancements
The PDF reader now supports six contrast options, and a cursor
can be displayed on the screen to highlight words.

Web browser enhancements
With its new webkit browser, Kindle 3 can zoom, fit page width to
the device, or display websites at actual size. It also features a text-
only Article Mode. Ah, doesn't that bring you back to the days of

28.8k modems?

Download Monitoring
Antsy readers can watch their books download in real-time.

Time Settings
The current time can now be set manually, handy when outside the
3G coverage area.

Full screen
The book header now auto-hides, leaving a bit of extra space for
text.

Two dictionaries
The Oxford Dictionary of English joins The New Oxford
American Dictionary for international support.

Alt-Del combo
Once again clear an entire line of text with ease.

The Kindle now sports its and audio and power controls and ports
along the bottom edge of the device, beside the shiny new
microphone.

10 MORE Ways To Use Your Kindle

If you already have a Kindle then you're probably aware of some of these features but if you're still unconvinced about how useful it can be, then read on.

Games
Two games are hidden as an easter egg in the device.
Just press Shift+Alt+M to open up a game of Minesweeper for you to play.
If you get bored of that, press M when you're playing to start a game of GoMoku, a more elaborate version of the game Xs and Os.

If you're based in the US, you can download games for the device which include games such as Blossom, a pipe-mania style game and Hidden Expedition, a point-and-click adventure. The monochrome display and the tiny keypad means that the games offered are somewhat limited but they'll definitely kill some time if you've nothing else to do.

* * *

Reading Comics & Manga

While there is a photo viewer for Kindle, a programmer has created a free app called Mangle (the name is a combination of Kindle and Manga) with a step by step guide to get it up and running. Since most manga (and some comics such as the Scott Pilgrim series) are published in black and white, it's the perfect medium for storing and reading them.

* * *

Personal notetaker

Again if you're in the US, for $0.99 you can download this kindle
app which allows you to jot down notes, ideas, lists, addresses,
numbers and many other things. There is a search function
allowing you to filter through existing notes and all files are saved
as .txt allowing easy accessibility and keeps the space needed to
save them to a minimum.

Image viewer

Well you can view them in monochrome but still the option is there. Just access your Kindle's memory through any computer and create a folder called 'pictures.' Add any .JPG, GIF or PNG images onto the file and disconnect.

When you power up your Kindle, Press Alt+Z to create an ebook featuring your photos for you to view. The principal is similar to the manga app that was mentioned earlier as to how you can view them. It's recommended not to load up images bigger than 600×800 as they take longer to load up.

Presentations and Flashcards

Since you can save word or PDFs onto your Kindle (after a little conversion work either through Amazon or yourself if you're familiar with the basics of HTML), it's the perfect way to keep your notes together and keep tabs of what you're saying if you're giving a presentation or talk.

On the other hand, if you want to use it to learn or study without bringing tonnes of notes, then you can save flash cards onto your Kindle. As you can rotate the screen display, you can look at it sideways. The best site to visit would be FlashCardExchange which allows you to easily create and use your own flashcards or download existing ones to learn.

Navigation

While it doesn't incorporates any GPS functions like its smartphone cousins, you can still use your Kindle to find your way around town. Just use google maps (maps.google.com/m/ directions) to find your way through text, just type in where you are and where you want to go and google will give you text directions to follow to get there.

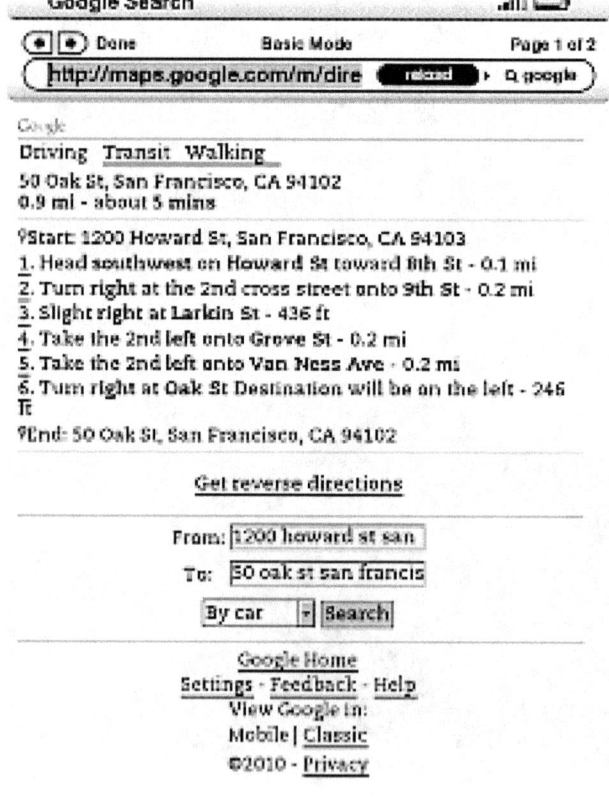

MP3 player & Text to Speech Reader

At the bottom of the Kindle, there is a headphone jack for you. Similar to the image viewer, just upload any MP3 files onto the kindle and you can listen to music while you're reading your favourite book.

Also if you're too lazy to read with your eyes, then use your ears instead by using the text-to-speech function. Just be sure that the book is modern as the program tends to have slight problems pronouncing olden words and for the most part ignores punctuation when reading through.

* * *

Web Browser

Select this item to launch We
choose a bookmark, or enter

Play MP3

Select this item to listen to mu
you read. Hold down the 'ALT
spacebar to stop or play, or th
next track. You must copy MP
computer to your Kindle's 'mu
feature.

Text-to-Speech

Start Text-to-Speech in the Tex
reading and your Kindle will st
allowed by the rights holder). H
and press the 'SYM' key to stor

Language Translator

If you're abroad and need an instant translator, then your Kindle can become a makeshift one. While you can access Google Translator, a much better translator can be <u>accessed through KindleFish which</u> is simpler and faster to use.
There's also a dialog option that allows you to enter a translation which switches every time it's used handy if you want to create a dialogue with someone and you trust them with your Kindle.

Dictaphone
Kindle 3 currently has a microphone at the bottom of the device (it's that tiny hole in between the headphone and USB ports) which officially has no use at the moment. However through some hacking, you can use it as a makeshift dictaphone, the instructions to do this <u>can be found on this forum where</u> you can download and modify it to record whatever you want. If it doesn't automatically scroll down, just search for 'Kindle Dictaphone' on the page.

* ALL the above information came from simplyzesty.com . Great website to browse .

How To do things the EASY WAY ?!

Rent textbooks through any Kindle

So Amazon has decided to give students a break and rent textbooks through any Kindle device or Kindle App.Here's a list of some of the great features this offers:

1.   Choose a rental length between 30 and 360 days and only pay for the exact time you need a book.

2.   Rent and read textbooks on PC, Mac, Kindle or your mobile device.

3.   Access any notes and highlights anytime, even after the rental expires!

4.

How does Kindle Textbook Rental Work?

You can rent for the minimum length (30 days) and save up to 80% off the list price. You can extend your rental by as little as 1 day as many times as you want and just pay for the added days. Download one of the free Kindle reading Apps by clicking here – you decide where you want to read your textbooks.

Search for your textbook in the Textbook Store or from the search bar. If a Kindle edition is available for rent, you'll see an option in the Formats section and select Kindle Edition.

On the Kindle Textbook page select the textbook rental end date. You only pay for the time you need and can extend or buy anytime.

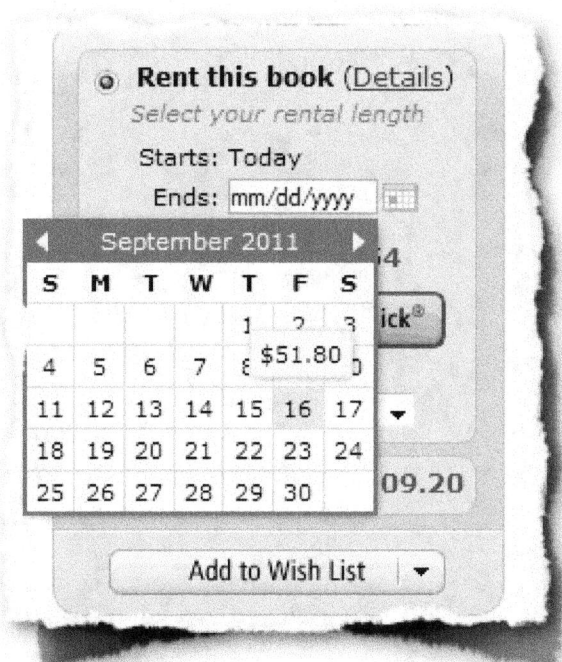

Finally, click on "Rent now with 1-Click" to place your order. What are your thoughts on this new way of acquiring textbooks for school?

* Information from kindlestuff.wordpress.com

How to Password Protect Your Kindle

To prevent others from using your Kindle or seeing your content, you can create a password that must be entered whenever your Kindle starts or wakes from sleep. If you forget your password, try looking at the password hint you entered when you first created the password.

Follow these simple steps to create a password:

1.   If you're not already on the Home screen, press the Home button.

2.   Press the Menu Button.

3.   Use the 5-way to underline "Settings" and press select.

4.   Use the 5-way to underline "turn on" next to the "Device Password" setting and press to select.

5.   Type in the password you want. The maximum password length is 12 characters.

6.   Navigate down and type in your password again to confirm.

7.   Navigate down and type in a hint. This hint can be displayed on the password entry screen to help you remember your password.

8.   Navigate down using the 5-way and select "submit".
And that's it! Now you can safely protect your Kindle from your curious family members .

* Information from kindlestuff.wordpress.com

How to Transfer MP3s to Your Kindle

You can transfer your MP3 files to Kindle by copying them to the "music" folder on your Kindle over USB. Kindle only supports MP3 audio files: AAC, WAV, MP3 with DRM and other music file formats are not supported.

To transfer MP3s to your Kindle, follow these steps:

1. Connect your Kindle to your computer, using the USB cable that came with the device.

2. You Kindle should appear on your computer in the same location you would normally find an external USB drive.

3. Open your Kindle. You should see a folder entitled "music." Drag any MP3s you'd like to play on your Kindle into this folder.

4. Using your computer, eject your Kindle from your computer.

For more information on playing background music while you read click here.

* Information from kindlestuff.wordpress.com

Let the Kindle Read to You with Text-to-Speech

You can turn on the application, Text-to-Speech, will will read aloud your books (where allowed by the book holder), newspapers, blogs, and personal documents. While reading a book or

periodical, press the Text key (Aa), then use 5-way controller to underline "turn on" for "Text-to-Speech". Press the 5-way to select "turn on". You can either listen through your Kindle's external speakers or plug in earphones into the headphone jack. While Text-to-Speech is playing, the screen will turn the pages automatically so you can follow along while the audio is playing. You have the choice of hearing your content spoken with a male or female voice and can also further optimise the listening experience by slowing down or increasing the rate of speech.
So there you have it, kick back and let the Kindle pamper you .

Play Background Audio While Reading

To play background audio (MP3 files) that you have transferred to your Kindle, follow the steps below:

1. If you are not already on the Home screen, press the Home button.
2. Press the Menu button.
3. Use the 5-way to navigate down until "Experimental" is underlined and press the 5-way to select it.
4. Use the 5-way to navigate down until "play music" is underlined and press down to select it.

The songs are played in order, by the date you added them to your Kindle. You can adjust the volume of the music using the volume controls on the bottom of your Kindle. You can continue to listen to the audio while reading content; the background audio continues to play unless you open an audio book, turn on text-to-speech, all of the files have been played, or if you stop the playback.

Tip: You can also play or stop background audio by holding down the Alt key (Alt) and pressing the space bar. You can forward to the next track by holding down the Alt key (Alt) and pressing the F key.

How to Use the Screen Rotation Feature

The Kindle screen image can be rotated so you can view the entire width of page. The buttons work the same in either rotation, but the 5-way controller movements are switched to match the rotation.

Follow these steps to lock your screen into landscape or portrait mode:

1. Press the Text key (Aa) located on the bottom row of the keyboard. Screen rotation is displayed at the bottom of the menu.

2. Move the 5-way to select one of the four options to lock the display in a set orientation: (1) portrait, (2) landscape with the keyboard on the left, (3) portrait with the keyboard on top, and (4) landscape with the keyboard on the right.

3. Press the 5-way to confirm your choice.

Note: You can view Kindle Store pages only in portrait mode.

How to Add Notes To Your Readings

Did you know you can add notes on what you are reading? Yes! Kindle stores all your notes for the current content in your annotations. You can view them at any time by pressing the Menu button and selection "View My Notes & Marks."

To add a note follow these steps:

1. Press Menu and choose "Add a Note or Highlight." This displays a blinking cursor.

2. Using the 5-way, move the cursor to the left of the word where you want to add your thoughts.

3. Type your note.

4. Using the 5-way navigate the cursor over "save note" and press the 5-way.

Notice the superscripted number where you inserted your note. Notes are numbered in the order they appear in the content, so if you later create another note on an earlier page, the numbering of the previously created notes will change.

How to Look Up Definitions

While reading a book, periodical, or personal document, you can see a brief definition of a word using the Lookup feature. The default dictionary is the The New Oxford American Dictionary included on your Kindle.

The Lookup Feature

To see the definition of a particular word in your reading content, follow these steps:

1. Press up or down on the 5-way controller to display the cursor. If you are zoomed in to a PDF page, you can also press Menu and choose "Place Cursor in Page" to display the cursor.

2. Use the 5-way to move the cursor in front of the word you want to look up.

3. If the word is found in the dictionary, a definition extract appears at the top or bottom of the screen.

4. To see the complete definition, press the Return key . You will now be placed in the dictionary and can use the Previous Page and Next Page to view other word definitions.

5. Press the Back button to return to your reading.

Get Organised by Creating Collections

You can create collections to personalise the way you organise your books, personal documents, and Audible books, and to make it easier to find items.

Creating a Collection

You can create as many collections as you need. To create a collection follow these steps:

1. If you are not already on the Home screen, press the Home button.

2. Press the Menu button and use the 5-way to select "Create New Collection".

3. Use the keyboard to enter the name of your collection. Press the Symbol key (Sym) to enter symbols and numbers.

4. Use the 5-way to select "save".

5. Your collection is created and displayed on the Home screen. The very first time you create a collection, the sort order changes to sort by collections on the Home screen. To change the sort order, move the 5-way up to underline "By Collections", and then move the 5-way to the right to choose another sort option.

Linking Your Kindle to Facebook and Twitter

If you are a not a member of social networks such as Twitter or Facebook, visit their website and create an account with them before you link your Kindle to them. They may require you to accept their terms of use before creating an account or using their service. The following steps describe the process for linking to your Twitter account, but you use the same process to link to other social network accounts.

To link your Kindle to your Twitter account, follow these steps:

1. If you are not already on the Home screen, press the Home button.
2. Make sure Whispernet is turned on.
3. Press the Menu button.
4. Use the 5-way to navigate to "Settings" and press to select it.
5. Press the Next Page to go to Page 3 of Settings.
6. Use the 5-way to navigate to "manage" next to the "Social Networks" setting and press to select. The "Manage Your Social Networks" screen appears.
7. To link your Kindle to your Twitter account, select "Link Account" under Twitter.
8. Use the 5-way to navigate to "Username or Email" and type your Twitter user name or e-mail address. To enter a capital letter,

press and hold the Shift key down while pressing the letter.

9. Use the 5-way to navigate to "Password" and type your password.

10. Use the 5-way to navigate to "Sign in" and press to select it.

11. If this is the first time you are linking your Kindle to your Twitter account, select Allow to confirm that you want to allow your Kindle to access your Twitter account.

There you have it! Start twitting away .

How to Send Personal Documents to Your Kindle

Kindle makes it easy to take your personal documents with you. Each Kindle has a unique and customisable e-mail address you can set on your Manage Your Kindle page. You can send unprotected Microsoft Word, PDF, HTML, TXT, RTF, JPEG, GIF, PNG, BMP, PRC and MOBI files to your Kindle e-mail address.

To access your personal documents on your Kindle, send attachments to your Kindle's e-mail address ("name"@free.kindle.com). The files will be sent to your Kindle via the Wi-Fi connection and also to the e-mail address associated with your Amazon account at no charge.

To have your PDF documents converted to Kindle format so you can take advantage of functionality such as variable font size, annotation, Text-to-Speech, etc., type "Convert" in the subject of the e-mail when you submit your personal document to "name"@free.kindle.com. Image-heavy PDF files are presented in landscape orientation and don't work with devices that have auto-rotation, so those will be delivered in the Kindle format.

You can also transfer personal documents to your Kindle at no charge using your USB connection.

How to Easily Publish your Blog on Amazon Kindle

Kindle Publishing for Blogs is a very easy to use publishing tool if you're interested in making your blog available on the Kindle. Kindle blog subscribers will pay a small fee to access blogs via the device, typically $1.99 a month per subscription. Amazon sets the price for each blog.

Amazon does make a massive 70% commission, while bloggers only earning 30%, however, you do get more exposure to your content, which can lead to more traffic and more ways for you to monetize.

Nevertheless, it's free to join and as with all things Amazon the process is very straightforward. Simply visit the Kindle Publishing for Blogs page and create an account. After you've done that follow these 10 easy steps:

1.   Add some personal and payment details (for when Kindle users subscribe to your blog).

2.   Add your URL or feed. Validation happens in a matter of seconds.

3.   Add a blog title, tagline, and description. Be descriptive and use keywords.

4.   Add the publisher or author's name.

5.   Add some visual elements. Add a blog screenshot. Add a banner, or logo, to identify your blog on the Kindle.

6.   Set your blog's language.

7.   Choose up to 3 categories and add a bunch of search keywords (you have up to 128 characters).

8.   Determine the frequency of posts.

9.   Preview and publish your blog.

10.   Wait for approval! If all works out you can expect to see your blog featured in the Kindle Store within 72 hours or less. There you have it. Now you can easily put your blog out there for everyone with a Kindle to see it. With over 500,000 Kindle users it's definitely worth publishing your content and maybe get paid for it.

Add Your Own Picture to the Kindle Screensaver

Add your own pictures to the Kindle to be used as the screensaver images that get rotated thru.

1.   Connect to your Kindle via USB.
2.   Create a folder named 'pictures'
3.   Within that new folder, create another folder name 'My Pictures'
4.   Copy any number of pictures you want into the new 'My Pictures' folder. 600×800 is the size of the screen display.
5.   On the Kindle, go to the Home Screen
6.   Press ALT+Z
7.   There should now be a 'book' named 'My Pictures' displayed.
8.   Open the 'book' to start the picture viewer.
9.   Cycle thru all of the pictures pressing F (to make them full screen), then ALT + Shift + 0 (the number zero) to select each one for the screensaver.

There you have it, enjoy your favorite pics. What are your thoughts on this neat feature?.

Use Your Kindle as a GPS Navigator

The Kindle might not have a GPS receiver, but it does have EV-DO that is location-aware. In the browser mode simple hit Alt-1. The Kindle will plot your current location on Google Maps. Just like on a PC, you can zoom into the street or zoom out and get a look at the surrounding area. Hit Alt-3 in the map and it will search for nearby restaurants. Then make sure to let the Kindle sit shotgun because selecting Alt-2 finds the nearest gas stations.

Playing Minesweeper from your Kindle

From the home menu, hold down Alt-Shift-M simultaneously to launch Minesweeper. Just like you play on your PC, the Kindle packs a full Minesweeper game. You use the I, J, K, and L keys to move up, left, down, and right, and ALT-Scroll to toggle from row to row or column to column. The M key lets you mark a mine and the Space key uncovers a cell.

Kinda cool that the Kindle has hidden features that allow to take a break from reading.

Playing Games on your kindle !

There are more than 100 games you can play on your Kindle , and the list is increasing even day . Click on the web address below and enjoy ..

http://www.amazon.com/tag/kindle%20game?ref_=tag_dpp_cust_itdp_t&store=1

Calendar Pro on your Kindle !

Calendar Pro allows you to create events, edit existing events, and view these events by day, month, or year. You can create multiple events within a day, month, or year, and events can overlap, be a full day in length, or extend for multiple days. Each event can also be personalised with a title, location, description, and time. Upcoming appointments are visible in the Agenda View, and you can quickly change the period you are viewing with the page turn buttons. It is easy to use, and each screen has a help page that describes controls and keyboard shortcuts.

Just another convenient tool Amazon has come up with. Wanna start getting organised click this link –> Calendar Pro to get it now .

Using Kindle lending Club !

Kindle Lending Club is a website that matches lenders and borrowers of Kindle ebooks. To participate in lending and borrowing Kindle books, you must first register as a user on the site or connect with Facebook Connect.

Lenders need to have access to a valid email address to loan a book, but it can be ANY valid email address. DO NOT use your Kindle's @kindle.com email address to register. There are many services that provide free email services and it's always handy to have an email address that is not associated with anything important when it might be accessible to strangers.

Kindle lending is a feature launched by Amazon. Any Kindle book that has lending enabled can be loaned by one Kindle user to another for 14 days. At the end of the loan period the title is automatically transferred back to the book owners Kindle. Each Kindle book you own can only be loaned once.

For more information on this website just click this link Kindle Lending Club

Playing Hangman Game on Kindle!

Hangman is a word puzzle game everyone played as a child, but with 600 puzzles of varying difficulty this game is no child's play. I remember playing this during class whenever my friends and I were bored. Now that it's available on Kindle, it gives me a break from reading and allows me to reminisce back to the old days . The objective is to complete the word or phrase in the least number of guesses. You are presented with a category that the word belongs to, as well as with a row of dashes representing the number of letters the word contains. As you suggest letters they are added in their correct positions, or if you guessed wrong, another body part is added to the figure hanging from a gallows. Guess the word or phrase before the figure is completed or you lose the game. You can get up to 2 hints per round and follow your progress with a running tally of your results.

Are you a Hangman pro? Click here to download it and challenge yourself!

Playing Sudoku Game !

Attention Sudoku Fans! EA has released a new Sudoku game for Kindle for $3.99 which includes wireless delivery.

EA Sudoku contains thousands of built-in puzzles, as well as the ability to enter and play a puzzle from your favorite newspaper or magazine in "Newspaper" mode.

With five difficulty levels from "Easy" to "Insane," Sudoku offers plenty of fun for Sudoku players of all skill levels. Built-in game features let you make "Notes," "Undo" moves, and apply "Error Checking." If you get stuck, you can use the "Hints" feature to fill out a cell for you, or use "AutoFill" to display the notes on all open cells on the game board. You can even track your game stats to see how you progress over time.

Are you a Sudoku addict? Download the game here.

Playing Solitaire Game !

Solitaire is now available on the Kindle for only $3.99 and contains 12 different modes of play–the Klondike game you know as well as 11 other variants: Pyramid, Yukon, Golf, Free cell, Wasp, Peaks, Canfield, Spinneret, Eliminator, Easthaven, and Baker's Dozen. It's a lot of card-game fun for both experts and novices alike.

This version of Solitaire comes with handy features such as a "Tutorial Mode" that will get you started on the different game play variants, optional in-game "Tips" as well as an "Auto-Move" feature that will help you out when you're stuck and don't know what to do next. For the Klondike game, there is even a "Vegas" mode to track your winnings in (virtual) dollars.

To buy and download the game click here –> Solitaire for Kindle

How to prevent Spam ?

To prevent spam, your Kindle will only receive documents from e-mail addresses you have approved on the Manage Your
Kindle page. Here is how you can set up your approved e-mail list:
1.   Visit the Manage Your Kindle page.
2.   Sign in to your Amazon account.
3.   Select "Personal Document Settings" from the left hand menu.
4.   Under the heading "Approved Personal Document E-mail List" select "Add a new approved e-mail address."
5.   Enter the e-mail address and select "Add Address."

Optimizing Kindle Browser !

While viewing articles on a web page, you can switch to Article Mode to make the text on the page easier to read. Article Mode makes reading articles more enjoyable by allowing you to focus on the main text on the page.

To switch to Article Mode, follow these steps:

1.	While viewing article on a web page, press Menu.

2.	Choose "Article Mode." The view switches to display the main article (including the article's text and images) on the page.

3.	Use the Next Page and Previous Page buttons to scroll up or down on the page.

4.	To return to the standard Web Browser view, press Menu and choose "Web Mode."

Disabling screen rotation on Kindle Fire !

If you're trying to read without having the screen rotate on you, here's a quick tip on how you can disable this feature on the Kindle Fire.

1. Go to Settings
2. You will see an Option that says Unlocked or Locked. If you tap it and keep it "Locked", it will disable the screen rotation feature. To enable screen rotation once again, tap it to the "Unlocked" position.

Adding a Bookmark to your Kindle Fire Browser !

If you have websites that you visit frequently or would just like easy access to a website without having to type in its address all the time, here's how to make a bookmark on the Kindle Fire's Silk Browser.

1. Open the Silk Browser and go to the page you want to bookmark
2. Tap the "Add Bookmark" icon at the bottom right area of the screen
3. Tap the page with the plus (+) sign
4. If you'd like you can edit the name of your bookmark. If not, you can just tap OK and you have just saved the website.

If you want to access all your bookmarks, just tap the bookmark icon at the bottom of your screen.

Getting 3G on the kindle Fire

Currently the Kindle Fire only supports Wi-Fi to access the internet or actions that require an internet connection. So what if you could get 3G signal on the Kindle using your smart phone? Here's how to do it:

(For this article I will discussing how to do this using an iPhone, but you can also do this with any smart phone hotspot)

iPhone

1. Go to Settings

2. Tap on Personal Hotspot and turn it "On"

3. You'll notice a Wi-Fi Password generated by your phone on the screen. You can use that one or personalise it by tapping on it.

4. Go to your Kindle Wi-Fi Menu and your iPhone's name should appear in the list of networks. (If it doesn't appear right away wait a few seconds)

5. You can then connect to it and use your phone's 3G on your Kindle Fire.

Converting EPUB files to Kindle Format

Even though the Kindle is currently not compatible with EPUB files, you can still use Google Book's EPUB files (which are free) and convert them to Kindle format. There are a couple of good ways to convert EPUB files into Kindle-compatible formats.

The first way to start converting EPUB files is to download Calibre (<– Click that link). Calibre is an e-reader client, e-library manager, but most importantly, an e-book converting machine!

The following is a list of the file types Calibre currently supports:
Input Formats: CBZ, CBR, CBC, CHM, EPUB, FB2, HTML, LIT, LRF, MOBI, ODT, PDF, PRC, PDB, PML, RB, RTF, TCR, TXT
Output Formats: EPUB, FB2, OEB, LIT, LRF, MOBI, PDB, PML, RB, PDF, TCR, TXTT

For Kindle owners the important input formats in that list are EPUB and the two comic-book formats CBZ and CBR. The important output formats are MOBI and PDF — either of which your Kindle can read without a problem. Calibre will sync these files to your Kindle, either through USB or by setting itself up as a server.

If you don't want to bother with Calibre, there's also RetroRead, a free site that converts EPUBs from Google Books to Kindle format.

Michael Haridy

Best Kindle Bloges !!

blog Kindle

Daily news about Kindle, eBooks, eInk and other related topics

On this blog you will track down the latest Amazon Kindle news. Blog Kindle will keep you up to date with whats hot in the bestsellers section, including books, ebooks and blogs... and will bring you great Kindle3 tips and tricks along with reviews for the latest KindleDX accessories.

Superb Web site . It is must have in your book marks . Some of the best tips and tricks we have in this book came from their site .

http://blogkindle.com/

KindleStuff

Everything you need to know about the Amazon Kindles .
One of the BEST if not the best website about Amazon kindles . It is a great site, full of information and instructions about how to do things with your Kindle .
You must bookmark it . The information you get from this site will enrich your use of your Kindle. Highly recommended .

http://kindlestuff.wordpress.com/

simply Zesty

Excellent up to date information web site . Highly recommended
to keep in your book marks .

http://www.simplyzesty.com/category/technology/

Kindle Ville Blog Spot

All About news, Opinions and Speculation about Amazon's
Kindle ebook Platform .
Good Blog full with many views, reviews .

http://kindleville.blogspot.com/

ireaderreview.com

Reviews of the latest free ebooks available and how to get access to them . Products review and opinions about their futures.

http://ireaderreview.com/

Kindle Formating

This website serves as a resource for authors, publishers, and anyone else who is interested in publishing content on the Kindle. For tips on how to format books for the Kindle, check out the Formatting section and the Frequently Asked Questions.

http://kindleformatting.com/index.php

Kindle Reader

Reading for enjoyment on your Amazon Kindle wireless reading device that is what this web site promote .

http://kindlereader.blogspot.com/

EduKindle

Great web site for using Kindle in education field.

http://www.edukindle.com/

… and at the end! WHAT is the future of Kindle?

TO answer that question !
What is better than to enter the mind of
 Amazon Kindle's creator Jeff Bezos !
Here is the excellent interview The Wire Magazine did with Jeff
Bezos on Nov. 2011.
http://www.wired.com/magazine/2011/11/ff_bezos/

Not the END

Not the end , it is the beginning of your journey with the eReader 'Kindle'. So … enjoy it .